Words of Faith

Words of Faith

Jesus Speaks Through the Saints

Edited by Craig Turner

TAN Books
Charlotte, North Carolina

Cataloging-in-Publication data on file with the Library of Congress.

Typeset by Lapiz Digital Services.

Cover design by Caroline Kiser.

Cover image: Bloch, Carl (1834-90). *Jesus Speaks with Samaritan Woman*, oil on copper plate, (Frederiksborg Palace Chapel, Copenhagen, Denmark).

ISBN: 978-0-89555-716-2

Published in the United States by
TAN Books
P.O. Box 410487
Charlotte, NC 28241
www.TANBooks.com

Printed and Bound in the United States of America.

A NOTE TO THE READER

The primary texts used in this book from which the visions were taken include:

Birgitta of Sweden: Life and Selected Writings (Classics of Western Spirituality), by Bridget of Sweden, edited by Marguerite T. Harris, Albert Tyle Kezel and Tore Nyberg (BS)

The Dialogue of St. Catherine of Siena, by Catherine of Siena, published by TAN Books. (CS)

A Tuscan Penitent: The Life and Legend of St. Margaret of Cortona, by Father Cuthbert, Burns Oats and Washbourne, London, 1900. (MC)

The page numbers in parentheses after each quote refer to the page or pages from which the quote was extracted. Quotes were used as they appear in the original works with the exception of some modernization of the usage of words. For example, "thee" and "thy" were updated to read "you" and "your."

ACKNOWLEDGMENTS

A NUMBER of different people deserve credit for their invaluable assistance in the production of this book. In addition to the research and work I did on this book, I must also recognize the people who compiled quotes from original sources and either researched or wrote biographies of particular saints. These people include:

Saint Bridget of Sweden
Kasandra Barker and Laura Brestovansky

Saint Catherine of Siena
Kathleen Lane and Tom Sherry

Saint Margaret of Cortona
Cathy Crisp and Tom Sherry

In addition, Bob French, who assisted with the editing of this work, gave important and useful editorial suggestions, as did Dawn Beutner, who assisted in a similar capacity. I would also like to give thanks to the Blessed Virgin Mary who intercedes for us in a variety of ways and never tires in her work on behalf of aching humanity.

"It is My will that the favors I have granted you, and shall yet grant, be announced abroad and published to the world."

—Jesus to Saint Margaret of Cortona

CONTENTS

Note to the Reader iii
Acknowledgments v
The Visionaries ix

Words of Faith

The Blessed 3
Chastity 5
Compassion 6
Confession 7
Contrition 9
Conversion 10
The Devil 18
The Eucharist 20
Expiation of Sin 24
Faith 25
God 30
Grace 33
Hell 38
Holiness 40
Hope 47
Humility 48

Jesus 50
Judgment 51
Justice 55
Love 56
Love of God 60
Love of Neighbor 63
Mary 65
Mercy 68
Mortal Sin 72
Obedience 73
The Passion of Christ 79
Peace 80
Penance 82
Poverty 83
Prayer 85
Priests 86
Purgatory 92
Sins 94
Spiritual Life 103
Suffering 109
Trials and Temptations 117
Virtue 121
Miscellaneous 122

THE VISIONARIES

THE book *Words of Faith* centers upon three souls whose intimacy with God is undeniably great. The majority of the conversations recorded deal with the spiritual life and the soul's relationship with God. But other matters are also addressed and recorded: prophecies that God gives to the recipient, explanations of certain events (either global or private), directions about when and where the recipient is to make a pilgrimage, etc. Each of these saints, just like each of us, has a unique story to tell. But often we find that saints do not tell their own stories. And so it is left to us to tell them.

St. Margaret of Cortona (1247–1297)

On the windswept hills of the Italian village of Laviano, surrounded by olive groves and small brooks descending the hills of Tuscany, Margaret of Cortona was born. Her mother died when she was only seven, and, devastated, she was then raised by her father and stepmother. The foster-mother held little, if any, affection for the little girl, and tragically, love was absent from Margaret's life. If it is true that cracks within marble later show upon its face, then the fractures in Margaret's love, too, would ultimately be revealed.

By the time she was seventeen she was stunningly attractive, a dazzling beauty with olive skin and dark hair, and it was to this beauty that a young cavalier, the son of a lord from a nearby region of Italy, induced a romance. She ran away with the man, partly to escape her home, and began a life of promiscuous living as she dwelled with him in his castle. For nine years she lived a life of luxury and opulence with the man, at times mocking the nearby villagers as she rode into town upon her handsome steed, declaring boldly that her licentious living and unchaste lifestyle were the best that one could hope for in life.

Margaret requested marriage to the man frequently, only to be rebuffed with a charming smile and a false promise that he would, one day, marry her. Nevertheless, she was perfectly content with her lifestyle. Thoroughly convinced that man's actions carry no consequences, she continued her indiscreet living, attended to by servants and ultimately bearing a son to the man of the castle. But her days of luxury were numbered, for one day the man's favorite hound returned to the castle without its master, and as it desperately indicated some sort of misfortune, Margaret followed the hound into the woods to the dead body of her lover. He had been murdered, possibly by thieves.

Utterly distraught and horrified, she returned to the castle and mourned the loss of her companion, reflecting upon her own life and her actions up to that point. She then quickly amended her life, returning all jewelry and property that had been given to her over the years. She left the castle with her little son and returned to her father's house, but the stepmother refused to keep her, and she was forced to leave. Adrift with a son and nowhere to turn, she heard faintly within her soul a voice that directed her to the small city of Cortona. She set off for the village, and after she arrived, two women came to her aid by providing her food and lodging, and ultimately introducing her to the Franciscans at the Church of San Francesco. It was here that she would begin her new life of devotion, prayer and penance.

For the first three years Margaret struggled with serious temptations. She was drawn to the frivolity of the world and the fleeting happiness of pleasures, and it was a great effort for her to overcome these feelings. But she fasted vigorously to quench the temptations, perpetually abstaining from meat and subsisting most of the time on bread and herbs.

After three years of probation, she became a Franciscan tertiary, and it was around this time that she was given the chance to beg in the streets of Cortona for her sustenance. She hardly looked upon this humiliation as a disgrace, because it not only provided her with a chance to grow spiritually, but allowed her the opportunity to become one of the poor, subsisting on alms. During this period, she began to experience the singular grace which today has made her famous: her visions, which were later dictated by her at the insistence of her spiritual directors and recorded for posterity. In 1277 she was in the local church of the Franciscans when she faintly heard the words: "What is your wish, poverella?" The voice, identified by her later as Jesus, addressed her with a word that means "little poor one." Margaret, reflecting upon the question, then responded, "I neither seek nor wish for anything but You, my Lord Jesus."

Jesus continued from this time to speak to Margaret—not simply through inspiration but with actual words—continuing to refer to her as "poverella." Around this time an unusual and singular event occurred in Margaret's life that, while already extraordinary in many ways, still deserves mention. Margaret's life followed the model of great penitents who came before her—the radical conversion, rejection of all worldly belongings, renunciation of attachments and even personal pleasures, and the subsequent reception of the highest mystical gifts. Yet, Margaret experienced one episode that is markedly different from nearly every other saint.

Though she was like many other famous penitents, one episode stands out as decidedly unique. Margaret asked Jesus one day why He called her "poverella," a term that might be addressed more to a stranger that one pitied than to an intimate friend. She requested that He refer to her as "My child," but for some months, despite her petitions, she was not granted the request. Then, one day while in prayer, as Margaret was insisting that Jesus refer to her as "My child," He told her that she must confess all her past sins in a general confession to receive this gift. She quickly asked that her conscience be enlightened to see all her past sins so that her confession would truly be comprehensive. Suddenly, her soul was flooded with divine light and enlightened with all the sins of her life, even those events that she had forgotten and therefore had never before confessed. When the Spirit of God had finished enlightening her soul, she sought out her confessor, Friar Giunta, a Franciscan, and engaged in a confession beginning with her earliest years that required eight days to complete! When her confession was finally complete, she attended the Holy Sacrifice of the Mass, and, upon receiving communion, heard Jesus call her with the sweetest tone of intimacy, "My child."

The voice of Jesus continued to speak to her throughout her life, giving her guidance and providing her with profound insights regarding the spiritual life, and it was from this point forward that she was blessed with greater mystical favors, including more frequent ecstasies. Twice during her life she was directed by Jesus to reprimand the local bishop, Guglielmo Ubertini Pazzi, because he lived more like a prince and soldier than an apostle of Jesus Christ. This same bishop was later killed in the battle of Bibbiena in 1289.

Margaret is honored today not only for the profound intimacy with which Jesus communed with her, but also for her work among the poor. She founded a hospital for the sick and poor, instituted a congregation of Franciscan tertiary sisters, established a confraternity of Our Lady of Mercy (the members vowed to help the poor and needy whenever they found them), and worked tirelessly as a peacemaker, intervening in civic feuds and conflicts.

Toward the end of her life she retired to the crumbling structure of the Church of Saint Basil, a hilltop ruin that overlooked the city. Though this fortress did not compare in stature to the castle she had left, and she had no servants to wait upon her nor jewelry to adorn her, she was nevertheless supremely happy. She undertook the restoration of the church, and it was here that she spent her last years, praying and fasting for the conversion of souls.

She died in 1297, her life having borne witness to the greatness of God's love and mercy, and her body was found later to be incorrupt, never having decayed. Like the glistening marble of a statue in the sun, her incorrupt body remains today a shining example of the miracles God performs for those who leave the world to find Him.

St. Bridget of Sweden (1303–1373)

Saint Bridget of Sweden, today honored as one of the patron saints of Europe, was born at the beginning of the fourteenth century into a family of wealth and means. Her father was one of the richest landowners in the country, both a lawyer and the governor of the province of Uppland. His realm was situated along the Baltic Sea just north of Stockholm, Sweden's capital. Bridget's mother, Ingeborg Bengstdotter, was also of the privileged class, and various members of her family served as second in command to Swedish King Magnus II during Bridget's lifetime.

Bridget's mother and father were both devoutly religious, and she was well grounded in piety and prayerfulness from their daily examples. At seven years of age she began to experience visions and mystical revelations, and they continued throughout her life, including one remarkable episode when the Blessed Virgin Mary appeared to her and placed a crown upon her head. Her mystical experiences included apparitions of Jesus, witnessing the birth of Jesus in Bethlehem, visions of purgatory and the reception of the "Fifteen Our Father and Hail Mary Prayers" given to her by Jesus to honor his wounds. She recorded many of the mystical experiences she had later in life in her book *Celestial Revelations*.

When Bridget was twelve years old her mother died, and she was faced either with marriage or entrance into a convent. Though she wanted to enter a convent, her father opposed the idea, and in 1316 at the age of thirteen, Bridget was given in marriage to Ulf Gudmarsson. Ulf, five years her senior, also came from an aristocratic and well-connected family, and though he was only a teenager, was prince of the land of Narke. Bridget immediately moved into his castle at Ulvasa in Ostergotland in the South of Sweden, also bordering on the Baltic Sea, and it was here that Bridget would spend much of her adult life.

Fortunately for Bridget, Ulf was also very devout in his faith. They had a good marriage and were blessed with eight healthy children, a rarity in a time when infant mortality was very high. Known throughout the land as a devoted mother to her four sons and four daughters, Bridget was also famous for her works of charity, especially toward Ostergotland's unwed mothers and their children.

Word soon spread throughout Sweden of Bridget's charitable good works and devout prayerfulness, and as a result she became a good friend of prominent theologians and priests. One of her closest friends, Nicolaus Hermanni, later became the bishop of Linkoping.

In the early 1340s Bridget and Ulf decided to make the lengthy and arduous journey to a famous medieval pilgrimage destination located in northwest Spain called Santiago de Compostela. A round trip journey such as this in the fourteenth century required two years of difficult travel by sea and over land as well as substantial financial resources. It also could be dangerous, as not only were thieves present along much of the journey, but diseases were equally plentiful.

Upon completion of the pilgrimage and while en route home, Ulf became ill, but recovered his health enough to finish the journey. When they arrived back in Sweden in 1343, both Ulf and Bridget decided to live in a monastery in a spiritual marriage without physical intimacy and divesting themselves of their worldly possessions. While this choice was unusual, even for more devout times during the Middle Ages, it was not unheard of. They lived in complete continence and devoted themselves to prayer and the works of the Cistercian monastery. The following year, while living in the monastery in Ostergotland, Ulf died of the disease he probably had contracted during his return from Spain.

Now a widow in her early forties, Bridget dedicated herself to prayer, asceticism and good works. By 1346 she had founded her own religious order, originally called the Order of St. Savior but later known as the Brigittines. The monastery was a "double order" for both men and women; the women devoted themselves to scholarship and study (very rare during her day) and the men to preaching and leading missions. Their chief monastery was located at Vadstena, in Ostergotland, a gift from King Magnus II.

Needing formal Church approval for her newly found order, Bridget set out for Rome with her daughter, Catherine (the future Saint Catherine of Sweden), to seek papal validation. As it turned out, she would never return to Sweden. Rather, she spent much of her time in Rome attempting to reconcile the major rifts in the Church that had caused the Pope to move his residence to the French city of Avignon. She urgently appealed to Pope Urban to return the Holy See back to Rome. The papacy eventually returned to the Eternal City, but not until 1377, four years after Bridget's death.

In 1372, Bridget, together with a son and daughter, set out on a pilgrimage to the Holy Land. The pilgrimage, though, was marred by shipwreck and the news of the death of one of her sons. When she returned to Rome, she continued her crusade to improve the moral climate of her age, even reprimanding rulers whom she found had become either corrupt or lax in devotion and piety. She died in Rome at the age of seventy, still working tirelessly to correct Church abuses and impress upon the people the need for personal holiness.

St. Catherine of Siena (1347–1380)

Saint Catherine was born into an age of instability, violence, schism and deep conflict in the life of the professed religious. The middle class was rising up to unseat the feudal nobility, the Pope was afraid to reside in Rome, families were fighting families in the streets and those in the religious houses were in a state of abject confusion regarding their loyalty to their family of origin or their vocation as religious.

Catherine was born on the Feast of the Annunciation of the Birth of Jesus, March 25, 1347, to Giacomo Benincasa, a cloth dyer, and his wife, Lapa. The family was pious, prosperous and large: it numbered twenty-five in all—twenty-three children with Catherine the youngest. Her twin, Giovanna, died at birth. Even though she was outgoing and considered to be the joy of the family, at the age of six Catherine resolved to be a hermit. She and her brother Stephen ran away from home to carry out this pursuit, but fear of upsetting their parents caused them to return home before the city gates were closed and they were locked outside the city walls.

Around this time Catherine also saw her first vision of Jesus, who gave her his blessing. At the age of seven she consecrated her virginity to Jesus through Mary, and was not to waver from this promise throughout her life despite opposition and many trials.

Although briefly indulging in what she called a "worldly life" for a period in her early teens, she led a hermit's life in her family home in her late teens and vigorously opposed an advantageous marriage her family had planned for her. She cut off her beautiful yellow hair and was made a servant in her own home. Only when her parents learned of her vow of chastity was she released from her family's ire and persecution. Also around this time she began to receive visitations and familiar conversations with Jesus, and after three years of these celestial experiences she was visited by Jesus who took her as His spouse, probably in the year 1366. She began her work serving the poor, tending the sick (especially the most destitute) and work for the conversion of sinners. She was able to live for long periods of time only on the Eucharist, and maintained a radiant and happy disposition though she was put through severe trials. She was blessed with great charm and gracefulness which aided her a great deal in her dealings with others.

During the summer of 1370 she went into a trance-like state close to death and was given visions of heaven, hell and purgatory. She was also given a command by God to leave her anchorite cell and work in the world. As a result, she was able to begin one of the most important labors of her life, the counseling and guidance of prelates and politicians on a number of matters related to both the Church and the world. Her work with the Pope gave her the opportunity to politely but frankly counsel him to leave his castle residence in Avignon and return the papacy to Rome. He did so in 1377, a move that profoundly affected the Catholic Church and returned the authority of the papacy to its rightful place.

She continued to experience mystical favors, though she neither sought them out nor requested them. It was around this time (in 1375) in her life that she was the recipient of the stigmata, the wounds of Jesus in the hands, feet, and side. In a typical act of humility, just as she was receiving the stigmata she implored the Lord to make the marks upon her invisible so no one would notice and think her favored or singular. Jesus quickly granted her request, and the stigmata remained invisible in her body until after she died.

It was also around this time that, while in Siena, Catherine dictated a long conversation between herself and God the Father, today referred to as *The Dialogue*. This long treatise is one of the most profound spiritual dialogues ever recorded, in which Catherine is privileged to ask questions of God the Father and hear His responses to her queries. Upon hearing His answers, she would speak the answers out loud with a scribe present in the room, and both the questions and answers were recorded for posterity. The locutions that are the subject of *Words of Faith* come from this long interlocution between Catherine and God.

Shortly after this time she began a long decline in health that culminated in her death. After a painful and mysterious agony that lasted three months, she died.

Saint Catherine of Siena believed that every person, and every Catholic in particular, possessed the ability to change the world. She believed that sanctity was not for only a few, but that the world needed saints in all corners and among all peoples. She worked tirelessly through her letter writing, evangelizing and speaking with common people, clergy, kings and even popes, to convey that each person is gifted with the ability to lead an extraordinary life of holiness. "If you are what you should be," she once said, "you will set the world on fire."

Words of Faith

The Blessed

God the Father said to Saint Catherine of Siena: "Fully converted souls would rather delight in the cross with Christ, acquiring it with pain, than to obtain eternal life in any other way." (CS, 181)

Saint Catherine of Siena was instructed by God the Father about how blessed souls obtain mental peace by accepting God's will: "No one born passes this life without pain, bodily or mental. Bodily pain My servants bear, but their minds are free, that is, they do not feel the weariness of the pain, for their will is accorded with Mine, and it is the will that gives trouble to man. . . . They bear everything with reverence, deeming themselves favored in having tribulation for My sake, and they desire nothing but what I desire. . . . I permit these tribulations through love, and not through hatred. And they who love Me recognize this. Examining themselves, they see their sins, and understand by the light of faith that good must be rewarded and evil punished. . . . [The blessed] deem themselves favored because I wish to [chastise] them in this life, and in this finite time. They drive away sin with contrition of heart . . . and their labors are rewarded with infinite good." (CS, 125–128)

God the Father spoke to Catherine about blessed souls who, in their journey to God, had renounced their own will and desires even to the point of embracing their sufferings: "As their will is not their own, but becomes one with Mine, they cannot desire [anything] other than what I desire. Though they desire to come and to be with Me, they are content to remain, if I desire them to remain, with their pain for the greater praise and glory of My name and the salvation of souls. In nothing are they in discord with My will. But they run their course with ecstatic desire, clothed in Christ crucified. . . . In as much as they appear to be suffering, they are rejoicing, because the enduring of many tribulations is to them a relief in the desire which they have for death. For often the desire and the will to suffer pain mitigates the pain caused them by their desire to quit the body. These not only endure with patience as I told you they did, but they glory through My name in bearing much tribulation. In this they find pleasure. Not having it they suffer pain, fearing that I do not reward their well-doing, or that the sacrifice of their desires is not pleasing to Me. But when I permit them many tribulations, they rejoice, seeing themselves clothed with the suffering and shame of Christ crucified. If it were possible for them to have virtue without toil they would not want it." (CS, 180–181)

God the Father said to Catherine: "[The blessed] are conformed so entirely to My will that they cannot desire except what I desire, because their free will is bound in the bond of love in such a way that, time failing them, and dying in a state of grace, they cannot sin anymore." (CS, 112)

God the Father said to Catherine: "Don't think that the happiness of the body after the resurrection gives more happiness to the soul. If this were so, it would follow that until they would have their body they would have imperfect happiness. This cannot be, because no perfection is lacking for them. So it is not the body that gives happiness to the soul, but [rather] the soul will give happiness to the body. The soul will give of her abundance and will re-clothe herself on the last day of Judgment in the garments of her own flesh which she has left. As the soul is made immortal, so the body in that union becomes immortal. . . . Understand that the glorified body can pass through a wall, and neither water nor fire can injure it." (CS, 112–113)

Chastity

Jesus said to Saint Bridget of Sweden: "Priests who have concubines and celebrate Mass are as acceptable and pleasing to God as were the inhabitants of Sodom whom God submersed in Hell. And even though the Mass, in itself, always is the same and has the same power and efficacy, nevertheless, the kiss of peace that such fornicating priests give in the Mass is as pleasing to God as the kiss by which Judas handed over the Savior of all. Therefore, constantly try as much as possible, with words and deeds—by enticing or rebuking or threatening—to work together with them so that they may endeavor to lead a chaste life, especially since they must touch so very holy a Sacrament, and with their hands, administer it to other faithful Christians." (BS, 178)

Jesus spoke to Bridget about people who wear provocative clothing and makeup: "The bodies of men and women are being deformed from their natural state by the unseemly forms of clothing that the people are using. And the people are doing this because of pride and so that in their bodies they may seem more beautiful and more lascivious than I, God, created them. And indeed they do this so that those who thus see them may be more quickly provoked and inflamed toward carnal desire. Therefore, know for very certain that as often as they daub their faces with antimony and other extraneous coloring, some of the infusion of the Holy Spirit is diminished in them and the Devil draws nearer to them. In fact, as often as they adorn themselves in disorderly and indecent clothing and so deform their bodies, the adornment of their souls is diminished and the Devil's power is increased." (BS, 209)

After being told by the Lord that she would be among the virgins of Heaven, St. Margaret of Cortona was astounded, asking, "Lord, how can this be with one so stained with sin?"

The Lord answered, "Your manifold sufferings shall cleanse your soul from all attraction to sin, and in your suffering and contrition you shall be restored to virginal purity."

Margaret then exclaimed, "O Christ, my Master, is Mary Magdalene among the virgins in the glory of Heaven?"

Jesus replied: "Except for the Virgin Mary and Catherine the Martyr, there is none among the virgins greater than Magdalene." (MC, 160–161)

Compassion

God the Father said to Saint Catherine of Siena: "When [a grace-filled person] sees something evidently sinful . . . he has true and holy compassion, interceding with Me for the sinner and saying with perfect humility: 'Today it is your turn, and tomorrow it will be mine unless the divine grace preserves me.'" (CS, 217)

God the Father said to Catherine: "[Perfectly converted souls] do not waste time in passing false judgments, either on My servants or on the servants of the world. They are never scandalized by any human murmurings. . . . They are content to endure anything for My name's sake. When an injury is done, they endure it with compassion for the injured neighbor and without murmuring against him who caused the injury." (CS, 217–218)

God the Father said to Catherine: "You should never judge the will of man in anything that you see done or said by any creature whatsoever, either to yourself or to others. . . . If you should see evident sins or defects, draw the rose out of those thorns—that is to say, offer them to Me with holy compassion. In the case of injuries done to yourself, judge that My will permits this in order to prove virtue in you and in My other servants. Assume that he who acts in this manner does so as the instrument of My will. Remember, too, that such apparent sinners may frequently have a good intention. No one can judge the secrets of the heart of man. That which you do not see you should not judge in your mind, even though it may externally be open mortal sin. See nothing in others but My will, not in order to judge, but with holy compassion." (CS, 219)

Confession

Jesus told Saint Catherine of Siena that in confession a soul receives the "Baptism of Blood" when the person has contrition of heart and confesses to a priest. The priests, He said, hold the keys of this Blood, and sprinkle it upon the face of the soul. Jesus continued to explain what happens when one does not participate in confession: "If the soul is unable to confess, contrition of the heart is sufficient for this baptism, the hand of My clemency giving you the fruit of this Precious Blood. But if you are able to confess, I wish you to do so. And if you are able to, and do not, you will be deprived of the fruit of the Blood. It is true that in the last extremity, a man desiring to confess and not being able to, will receive the fruit of this baptism." (CS, 173)

God the Father said to Catherine: "You see, then, that these baptisms [i.e. confession] which you should all receive until the last moment are continual, and though the pains of the Cross were finite, the fruits of them which you receive in baptism, through Me, are infinite." (CS, 173)

Jesus said to Saint Bridget of Sweden: "When there is a fire in the house, it is necessary to have a vent hole through which the smoke can go out so that the inhabitant may enjoy the warmth. Thus, for everyone who desires to keep My Spirit and My divine grace, frequent confession is useful so that through it, the smoke of sin may escape. For although My divine Spirit is in itself unchangeable, nevertheless it quickly withdraws from the heart that is not guarded by humble confession." (BS, 132)

An angel told Bridget about the graces Bridget's son received at death: "This [man's forgiveness] was done by his mother's tears and long labors and many prayers. God sympathized with her sighs and gave to her son this grace: namely, that for every sin he committed, he obtained contrition, making a humble confession out of love for God. Therefore those sins have been blotted out." (BS, 184)

Fra Filippo was a confessor who was afraid to question penitents who hid their sins from him in confession. He asked Saint Margaret of Cortona through her confessor to ask the Lord to advise him about what to do. When Jesus heard her prayer, He said to her: "Tell Fra Filippo in My name that he can safely hear confessions and question his penitents. There are diversities of graces among men. This grace of hearing confessions and questioning penitents is granted to him because of his purity of mind and body."

She was also told, "If a thousand people should come to confession to him in one day, he must not refuse to hear one of them, nor fail to question anyone whom he has reason to think needs questioning. Sinners often do not confess their sins because, in the blindness of mind which sin brings upon them, they do not see their sin. This is their own fault, since by the evil odor of their lives they have driven Me away, I who am the true light.

"It therefore becomes necessary, My child, that confessors should question sinners concerning their sins. I love the Friars Minor because of this; they have a zeal and holy solicitude for souls, and by their labors [they] bring back many souls to life."

Our Lord also gave Margaret advice concerning another friar, Benigno. He was in doubt about how frequently he should say Mass. Jesus advised: "Tell Fra Benigno, who is afraid to receive the Sacrament of My Body and Blood too frequently, that I permit him to celebrate frequently. However, before he goes to the altar, have him make a full confession of all his sins and [have him] cast out all disturbances in his soul. I command him to persevere to the end in that compassion for the poor which he now has. It pleases Me very much that he goes out seeking the poor, the sick, and the ailing in their own homes." (MC, 271–273)

Contrition

Jesus said to Saint Bridget of Sweden: "Come and rise quickly through penance and contrition. Then I will forgive your sins and give you patience and strength to be able to withstand the plots of the Devil." (BS, 40)

The Virgin Mary said to Bridget: "You should be like a mirror, clear and clean, and like a sharp thorn: a mirror through honest and godly behavior and through good example, but a thorn through denunciation of sinners." (BS, p. 97)

The Virgin Mary said to Bridget: "Say to my friend the friar, who although you sent his supplication to me, that it is the true faith and the perfect truth that if a person, at the Devil's instigation, had committed every sin against God and then, with true contrition and the purpose of amendment, truly repented these sins and humbly, with burning love, asked God for mercy, there is no doubt that the kind and merciful God Himself would immediately be as ready to receive that person back into His grace with great joy and happiness as would be a loving father who saw returning to Him His only, dearly beloved son, now freed from a great scandal and a most shameful death. God Himself forgives His servants all their sins if they assiduously repent and humbly ask Him for mercy and they fear to go on committing sins, and, with all the longing of their hearts, desire God's friendship above all things." (BS, 169)

Conversion

During the time that Saint Margaret of Cortona was busy with her neighbors' affairs, she was deprived of her accustomed intimacy with God. She sought Jesus in great sorrow and He answered her, saying: "Margaret, you seek Me among things of the earth, busying yourself with things of this life; therefore when you find Me it is amidst things of the earth. If you wish to seek Me in My Heavenly kingdom, keep your mind fixed on the things of Heaven, and you will find the spiritual comfort you are seeking. For the things of this world prevent you from living the life of the Spirit."

Margaret replied, "But, Lord, am I not separated from the world and yet I do not serve You?"

Jesus said, "When you are hidden from the world, it is true that interior temptations assail you. Yet it is safer to struggle with these temptations than to seek security in intercourse with the world, for temptation purifies the soul. When your mind is crowded with earthly affairs, the dwelling I have prepared for Myself in your heart is closed against Me." (MC, 118–119)

The Virgin Mary said to Saint Bridget of Sweden: "Daughter, you must have five inward and five outward things. First outwardly: a mouth clean of all detraction, ears closed to idle talk, modest eyes, hands busy with good works, and withdrawal from the world's way of life. Inwardly, you must have five things: namely, fervent love for God, a wise longing for Him, the distribution of your temporal goods with [the] right intention and, in a rational way, humble flight from the world, and a long-suffering and patient expectation of My promises." (BS, 105)

When Bridget was in Jerusalem on pilgrimage, she didn't know whether it would be better for her to lodge in the monastery of the Franciscans, or to stay at the common hostel as a good example to other pilgrims. The Virgin Mary appeared to her while she was in prayer and said: "In that place on Mount Zion there are two kinds of human beings. Some love God with all their heart. Others want to have God, but the world is sweeter to them than God is. And therefore, so that the good may not be scandalized and so that you may not give an occasion to the lukewarm or [future generations], it is therefore better to reside in the place appointed for pilgrims." (BS, 194)

Margaret was shown her future place in Heaven, and she had no words to speak of the beauty except: "O great Lord! If this place were given to one of Your very apostles, even so the whole Heavens would be astonished. How much more then, if it be given to me who am only but a darkness of sin?"

Then she heard Jesus say to her: "My child, now may you openly tell and proclaim that you are My chosen one and My true child."

Another day, Jesus told Margaret that He makes the small things great and the worthless precious, and that He chose her out of the abyss to be His. Upon hearing this, Margaret exclaimed, "My Lord Jesus Christ, let me retire altogether from the world, for I live in continued doubt of my own constancy. But if you will deign to separate me from the world, I shall no more fear lest I be parted from Your mercy."

The Lord comforted Margaret saying, "My child, you are already confirmed in grace and sanctified in soul and body because of your true faith and fervent desire and of your pure intention in every thought, word, and deed; nor will I ever permit you to be separated from Me, but I will honor you both in life and after death."

Still dwelling upon her own unworthiness to commune so intimately with the Lord, Margaret then said to Jesus, "Lord, how can You bestow such high favors upon one so vile?" *The Lord answered,* "Because I have made you as a net to catch fish in the ocean of the world. Hence My promises to you are not for your sake alone, but for the sake of My people who shall be led back to Me. Therefore is it My will that the favors I have granted you, and shall yet grant, be announced abroad and published to the world." (MC, 156–159)

One Sunday, although Margaret received Holy Communion with great reverence, her spirit sank immediately afterwards and all joy left her. She determined to seek out Christ so she could have some relief. Leaving her home she began calling aloud for Him, and was soon taken in spirit to the feet of Jesus. Like Mary Magdalene, Margaret washed Jesus's feet with her tears, and afterwards wiped them. She then begged Our Lord that she be allowed to see His Face. But Jesus said to her: "You cannot look upon My Face and see Me as I am until you are placed in the glory of the Blessed. Though your Lent be prolonged now, yet know that your Easter will surely come."

Margaret asked Jesus if He approved of her mentioning the great favors she received from Him while she was in the presence of those who accompanied her. Jesus answered: "It is My will that you should declare these favors when you are in a state of ecstasy and are unaware of their presence." (MC, 222)

While praying one day, Margaret heard a voice informing her to prepare herself for the coming of Jesus, who wished to commune with her intimately. Through her the Lord would send forth loving kindness into the world. Margaret always balked in the face of praise and begged Jesus: "Lord, if it pleases You, I will not speak of this to my confessor, the friar."

But Jesus told her: "Tell your confessor and the other friars that they are to hold you hidden from the world. And you yourself hide from the world as far as you are able. You wish too much to dwell apart [from the world] in the enjoyment of My consolations, forgetful of what you owe to My children. I could easily have called you to walk alone in secret and have led you this way to the kingdom of Heaven if I had so willed. But such was not My will."

Margaret told Jesus: "Lord, I know I have offended [You] by my lack of charity. Yet, it was from mere thoughtlessness, not from lack of desire. In my heart I desire and pray unceasingly that You would grant [sinners] full mercy."

Jesus responded to her: "Have I not told you that you are placed in the world to be a light to the blind? Whoever has charity toward My children has charity toward Me. And now I would have you tell My sons, the friars, that when they preach they are not to talk about the birds of the air or otherwise vainly. Rather, let them preach the words of the Gospels and Epistles. They should not care if people murmur against them, for they also murmured against Me, their Lord. Again, tell the friars that I have given them larger nets and greater power in preaching the Gospel than I have given to other preachers. Therefore, I command them to preach about My sufferings and death to the people. And when they preach, let them suffer in their own souls as I suffered. In this manner they will turn sinners away from sin and draw them onwards to that blessed delight which I purchased for them at so great a cost. Hell has sent forth new legions to stir up the world, and preachers must be fervent and full of zeal."

One morning Margaret asked Jesus for the grace to feel to a greater degree the enjoyment of His presence. Jesus said to her: "You ask great things. But are you worthy of them?"

Margaret answered Him: "My Lord Christ, I am not worthy. Yet I still have recourse to Your pity."

Jesus then said to her by way of admonishment: "This hunger [you have] for the enjoyment of My presence is simply the sign of a weak soul. You must think of others, the children of My redemption. For such graces as I have given you are not for your own sake alone, but for the sake of those who still crucify Me. Yet in My fatherly love for them I humble Myself so that I may bring them back to Me. But you care about nothing except satisfying your own hunger, and you are forgetful of the children for whose sake I have established great deeds in you."

Margaret responded humbly: "My Lord, if it is for the greater good of Your children, lead me back to the early days when You spoke to them through me. But I fear, my Lord, that You have become my confessor. So to You, O Eternal Priest, I accuse myself of all my negligences." And right away she began accusing herself of her faults.

But Jesus said: "No, not to Me alone should you confess your faults, but [tell them] to your confessor also. Remember the lepers and how I sent them to the priests to be cleansed."

One day, Jesus said to Margaret: "In order to keep careful guard over yourself you have to separate yourself from the world."

Margaret cried out: "But Lord, even when I separate myself from the world I serve You badly."

Jesus responded to her: "It is better to struggle against the temptations from within yourself than to flee from them and keep company with the world, for in your struggles with yourself your soul is purified. But if you linger in the world, your mind becomes busy with vain thoughts. Then, when I come to seek rest in your soul I find it already occupied and its purity dimmed. You [no longer] live the daily life of suffering with Me which sinners inflict upon Me."

At this point Margaret was shown definitively all her faults and those occasions when she had offended God. Since she no longer enjoyed the consolations of her earlier days, she asked: "Lord, why is it I am no longer aware of the joys of Your kingdom?"

"I deal with you as I find you." *Jesus said,* "Right now your mind is almost wholly taken up with the affairs of those who come to you."

When Margaret requested to retire into solitude, Jesus continued: "Now I am indeed to you a father. But you are not a child to Me."

Margaret answered: "Truly, Lord, I do know that it is for the sake of Your children that You bestowed on me such immense favors. It is You who are the joy of angels and the delight of the blessed." *Her soul was then filled with such a consolation that she felt nothing except pure joy. She then continued:* "Lord, so great is the joy I find in Your presence that in comparison all things in Heaven and on earth pass into nothing. As soon as You are near [me] all trouble vanishes and I learn things no words can utter. O Lord, You are an unquenchable fire. I desire to be enkindled by You, and I pray that I could know how great is Your love for me."

The Lord again gently scolded Margaret, saying, "Can you think of nothing but yourself?"

Margaret responded: "My Lord, since You said this hunger in my soul is a sign of weakness, I beg you to make me strong."

Jesus answered her: "I've already given you a strengthening medicine which you have used very little—namely, that you should cast out your fears and rein in your desires. For love of Me do not be so solicitous about your body. You want a perpetual Easter, but [first] you have to endure a Lenten fast." (MC, 245–247; 253–257)

One Sunday during the Easter season, Margaret begged the Lord to come to her in spirit. Jesus said to her: "What do you want, my child? Do not fear, for I, your Creator, am with you."

Margaret became timid and felt she was unworthy to say anything, so Christ invited her to ask for a blessing in the name of the Eternal Father. When she requested this blessing, Jesus said: "I, your Lord, bless you in all your works."

Margaret, being very humble, inquired: "What are my works, O Lord?"

Jesus answered her: "My child, your eating and drinking, your waking and sleeping, your silence and your speaking, and all your life is a prayer in My sight, because of your desire to serve Me and your fear of offending Me." (MC, 284–285)

Saint Catherine of Siena was known to experience mystical favors that astonished witnesses who were present. On one occasion, after receiving Holy Communion, she felt weak and was taken back to her cell where she possessed a bed composed of a simple plank of wood. According to her confessor and biographer, Blessed Raymond of Capua, after being laid down on her bed, her body "rose into the air and remained there without anything supporting it, as three witnesses I shall name claim to have seen. Finally, she came down again onto the bed, and then in a very hushed voice she began to utter words of life that were sweeter than honey, and so full of wisdom that they made all the people there cry."

Despite this tremendous gift, she always would strive for greater sanctity. God the Father spoke to her on a different occasion about striving for perfection: "The soul is never so perfect in this life that she cannot attain to a higher perfection of love. My only-begotten Son, your Captain, was the only one who could not increase in perfection because He was one with Me and I with Him. Therefore His soul was blessed through union with the divine nature. Be sure that you . . . are always ready to grow in greater perfection . . . by means of My grace." (CS, 196)

The Devil

God the Father said to Saint Catherine of Siena: "[The damned] see [the Devil] in his own form, which is so horrible that the heart of man could not imagine it. . . . If you remember well, you know that I showed him to you in his own form for a little space of time, hardly a moment, and you chose after you had returned [to your own consciousness] rather to walk on a road of fire, even until the Day of Judgment, than to see him again. With all this that you have seen, even then you do not know very well how horrible he is. By Divine justice he appears [even] more horrible to the soul who is deprived of Me, and more or less according to the gravity of her sin." (CS, 106)

God the Father said to Catherine: "No one should fear any battle or temptation of the Devil that may come to him, because I have made My creatures strong, and have given them strength of will, fortified in the Blood of My Son." (CS, 118–119)

God the Father said to Catherine: "I have told you that the Devil invites men to the water of death. That is, [he invites them] to that which he has, and blinding them with the pleasures and conditions of the world, he catches them with the hook of pleasure under the guise of good. He could catch them in no other way—they would not allow themselves to be caught if they saw that no good or pleasure to themselves could be obtained in this manner. For the soul, by her very nature, always relishes good. Yet, it is true that the soul, blinded by self-love, does not know and discern what is true good and profitable to the soul and to the body. So the Devil, seeing them blinded by self-love, iniquitously places before them diverse and various delights, colored so as to have the appearance of some benefit or good. He gives to everyone according to his condition those principal vices to which he sees him to be most disposed." (CS, 121–122)

God the Father said to Saint Bridget of Sweden: "Although the Devil lost the dignity of his previous rank, he did not lose his knowledge, which he possesses for the testing of the good and for his own confusion." (BS, 130)

God the Father said to Bridget: "The Devil is, as it were, the lictor and the examiner of the just. Therefore, with My permission, he vexes the souls of certain people, he overshadows the consciences of others, and of some he vexes even the bodies." (BS, pp. 146–147)

God said to Bridget: "The Devil and I do struggle, in that we both desire souls as bridegrooms desire their brides. For I desire souls in order to give them eternal joy and honor, but the Devil desires souls to give them eternal horror and sorrow." (BS, 174)

Jesus said to Saint Bridget: "I am the Creator of all and Lord over the devils as well as over all the angels, and no one will escape My judgment. The Devil, in fact, sinned in a threefold manner against me: namely through pride, through envy, and through arrogance. He was so proud indeed that he wished to be lord over Me and that I should be subject to him. He also envied Me so much that, if it were possible, he would gladly have killed Me in order to be lord himself and sit on My throne. Indeed, his own will was so dear to him that he cared nothing at all about My will so long as he could perform his own will. Because of this, he fell from Heaven, and, no longer an angel, he became a Devil in the depths of Hell." (BS, 208)

Saint Margaret of Cortona prayed: "The deceiver of souls redeemed by You has wickedly told me that if in my accustomed way I seek You so fondly, I shall become mad." *Christ replied,* "Truly, My child, have you called him the deceiver of souls. But have no fear: you are My little plant, and I am He who planted you. Follow Me, for I am your guide whom you desire with a pure heart."

The Eucharist

Saint Catherine of Siena's biographer, Blessed Raymond of Capua, wrote frequently about her love of God and her immense love for the Holy Eucharist. The ecstasies she experienced were often after having received the most holy Body, Blood, Soul and Divinity of Jesus in Holy Communion. Blessed Raymond wrote about her love for Jesus in the Blessed Sacrament in this way: "Seeing or receiving the Sacrament of the Altar always generated fresh and indescribable bliss in her soul, so that her heart would very often throb with joy within her breast, making such a loud noise that it could be heard even by her companions. At last, having noticed this so often, they told her confessor [at the time] Fra Tommaso about it. He made a close inquiry into the matter and on finding it was true, left the fact in writing as an imperishable record." *Catherine herself testified that her bliss was so great, particularly when she received communion, that she felt as if she might not continue living.* "My mind," *she said,* "is so full of joy and happiness that I am amazed my soul stays in my body."

God the Father said to Catherine: "Oh, dearest daughter, open well the eye of your intellect and gaze into the abyss of My love. For there is no rational creature whose heart would not melt for love in contemplating and considering, among the other benefits she receives from Me, the special gift that she receives in the Sacrament [of the most holy Eucharist]. With what eye, dearest daughter, should you and others look at this mystery? How should you touch it? Not only with the bodily sight and touch, because in this sacrament all bodily perceptions fail. The eye can only see and the hand can only touch the white substance of the bread. The taste can only taste the savor of the bread. The bodily senses are deceived. But the soul cannot be deceived in her perceptions unless she wishes to be—that is, unless she lets the light of the most holy faith be taken away from her by infidelity. How is this sacrament to be truly tasted, seen and touched? With the sentiment of the soul." (CS, 234–235)

Jesus said to Catherine: "You cannot receive the Body without the Blood, or the Blood or the Body without the Soul of the Incarnate Word, nor the Soul, nor the Body without the Divinity of Me, the Eternal God, because none of these can be separated from each other. As I said to you in another place, the Divine nature never left the human nature, either by death or from any other cause. So, you receive the whole Divine Essence in that most sweet Sacrament concealed under the whiteness of the bread, for as the sun cannot be divided into light, heat and color, the whole of God and the whole of man cannot be separated under the white mantle of the host. For even if the host should be divided into a million particles—if it were possible—in each particle I would be present, whole God and whole Man." (CS, 230)

Regarding the Sacrament of the Eucharist, God the Father told Catherine: "You personally participate in this light, that is, in the grace which you receive in this Sacrament, according to the holy desire with which you dispose yourselves to receive it. He who should go to this sweet Sacrament in the guilt of mortal sin will receive no grace, though he actually receives the whole of God and the whole of Man. Do you know the condition of the soul who receives unworthily? She is like a candle on which water has fallen which can do nothing but crackle when brought near the flame, for no sooner has the fire touched it than it is extinguished, and nothing remains but smoke." (CS, 232)

Regarding a soul that receives Holy Communion in a state of grace, God the Father said: "See, dear daughter, in what an excellent state is the soul that receives, as she should, this Bread of Life, the Food of the Angels. In that soul grace dwells, for, since she has received this Bread of Life in a state of grace, My grace remains in her after the accidents of bread have been consumed. . . . There also remains in you the wisdom of My only begotten Son, by which the eye of your intellect has been illuminated to see and to know the doctrine of My Truth, and, together with this wisdom, you participate in My strength and power. . . . " (CS, 238–239)

Every time Saint Margaret of Cortona approached the altar to receive communion, she was so moved by her feelings of unworthiness that she trembled in all her body. One day she exclaimed: "My Lord, do I offend You by my insatiable hunger for You in Holy Communion?"

Our Lord answered: "No, but it pleases Me much. And for this I bless him who is your confessor and staff, and I give him a special grace because he has counseled you to communicate often, and has comforted you in your doubt. Fear not. Whatsoever I have promised you, and whatever you ask of Me, whether at your meditation or at any other time, I shall sweetly listen to and grant." (MC, 149)

There was an unnamed lay brother who was well loved by his brothers and also by God. He sought so much to pray that all his other activities were as a heavy weight on his shoulders. He wanted only to recite the Divine Praises, to listen to sermons and to pray. He also desired to receive Holy Communion more frequently and asked Margaret to pray to the Lord about this.

Jesus responded to Margaret: "My child, tell the brother that he is to receive Me, his Creator, once every fifteen days; such is My pleasure. I do not say this because of any notable defects in him, but rather that he may thirst the more for Me and receive Me the more hungrily.

"When at any time he desires to receive Me and is not able to, let him remember the words of the holy Doctor of the Church who said: 'Believe and you have eaten.' Therefore, have him prepare his soul for new graces and strive to amend his faults and to cast out all sin.

"Wherever he may be, whether in the dormitory or the cloister, in the kitchen or the refectory, or in any other place, let him always keep My Cross before his soul. Let him be crucified with Me. From this fountain shall flow forth for him not only the graces he prays for, but other [graces] he might well pray for. And let him take comfort, because the time will come when he shall [receive Holy Communion] every day. At that time he will no longer serve in the kitchen." (MC, 234; 236; 278–279)

At the elevation of the Eucharist during Mass one day, Saint Bridget of Sweden saw in the hand of the priest a young man of extraordinary beauty, who said, "I bless you who believe; to those who don't believe I am a judge." (BS, 46–47)

Expiation of Sin

God the Father told Saint Catherine of Siena: "Do you not know, dear daughter, that all the sufferings which the soul endures, or can endure, in this life, are insufficient to punish one smallest fault? The offense done to Me, the Infinite Good, calls for infinite satisfaction. However, I want you to know that not all the pains that are given to [human beings] in this life are given as punishments, but as corrections. This is to chastise a [person who offends]. Yet, it is true that both the guilt and the penalty can be expiated by the desire of the soul, by true contrition, not through the finite pain endured, but through the infinite desire. God, who is infinite, wishes for infinite love and infinite grief." (CS, 30–31)

God the Father told Catherine: "I give [My] Blood and use it for salvation and perfection in the case of the man who disposes himself properly to receive it. It gives life and adorns the soul with every grace in proportion to the disposition and affection of him who receives it. It also gives death to him who receives it unworthily, living in iniquity and in the darkness of mortal sin." (CS, 66)

God the Father said to Catherine: "[Jesus] was man's foster mother, who with the greatness and strength of the Deity united with your nature, endured the bitter medicine of the painful death of the cross to give life to you little ones debilitated by guilt." (CS 69)

God the Father said to Catherine: "The endurance of suffering alone, without [contrition for the sins committed], is not sufficient to punish a fault." (CS, 45)

Faith

The Friars Minor [Franciscans] were holding their Provincial Chapter in Siena [thought to be in the year 1288]. Some of the friars began arguing that Saint Margaret of Cortona's visions of Jesus were possibly delusions, or perhaps even frauds, and that she purposely created them to win the praise of the people. This troubled and saddened Margaret. Jesus came to her and asked, "Why are you weeping?"

She answered: "My Lord, You know all things even before they happen. You know why I weep and that I cannot do otherwise. I have to struggle against foes who fight against me—the friars to whom You commended me now terrify me by their doubts concerning me."

Jesus responded to her: "My child, don't be astonished if some of the friars have doubts about you and argue against you, for so it was with Me, the Son of the Living God. Some believed in Me and others doubted Me." (MC, 187)

"My Lord," *said Margaret one day,* "I confess truly that it is paradise to be in Your presence. Yet even so I do not believe that one can have enough of You or that a fullness of You will not produce hunger even in the paradise of the blessed. For the infinite joy of those who taste You draws souls ever more and more to You."

Then Jesus asked Margaret: "Do you firmly believe and confess that the Father, Son, and Holy Spirit are one God?"

"Yes, Lord," *Margaret replied,* "and since I firmly believe that You are one in substance and three in persons, please grant me perfect security concerning your promises."

But Jesus replied to her: "My child, this perfect security which you seek, you cannot have until I place you in the glory of My kingdom."

Upon hearing this Margaret boldly responded: "Lord, did You keep Your saints in fear and doubt the same way You are now doing to me?"

Jesus answered Margaret: "I gave strength to My saints in their sufferings, but they did not have perfect security until they came into My kingdom." (MC, 200–201)

God the Father told Saint Catherine of Siena: "I say to you all that you should ask, and it will be given you. For I deny nothing to him who asks of Me in truth." (CS, 38–39)

God the Father said to Catherine: "A man more readily sees spots on his face when he looks in a mirror. So [too] the soul who with true knowledge of self, rises with desire and gazes with the eye of the intellect at herself in the sweet mirror of God knows better the stains of her own face by the purity which she sees in Him." (CS, 62)

God the Father said to Catherine: "The soul can, by her free will, make a choice either of good or evil, according as it pleases her will. So great is this liberty that man has, and so strong has this liberty been made by virtue of this glorious Blood, that no demon or creature can constrain him to one smallest fault without his free consent." (CS, 70)

God the Father said to Catherine: "[Jesus'] doctrine—of which I have spoken to you, and which was confirmed by the apostles, declared by the blood of the martyrs, illuminated by the light of Doctors, confessed by the confessors, narrated in all its love by the evangelists, all of whom stand as witnesses to confess the Truth—is found in the mystical body of the Holy Church." (CS, 86–87)

God the Father said to Catherine: "Even though I created you without your help, I will not save you without it." (CS, 251)

God the Father told Catherine: "All consolations are thorns that pierce the soul who loves them disordinately." (CS, 141)

Regarding good and holy souls that have yet to reach perfection, God the Father told Catherine: "There are some who have become faithful servants, serving Me with fidelity without servile fear of punishment, but rather with love. This very love, however, if they serve Me with a view to their own profit or the delight and pleasure which they find in Me, is imperfect. Do you know what proves the imperfection of this love? The withdrawal of the consolations which they found in Me, and the insufficiency and short duration of their love for their neighbor, which grows weak by degrees and oftentimes disappears. Toward Me their love grows weak when, on occasion, in order to exercise them in virtue and raise them above their imperfection, I withdraw from their minds My consolation and allow them to fall into battles and perplexities. This I do so that, coming to perfect self-knowledge, they may know that of themselves they are nothing. . . . At such a time these weak ones of whom I speak relax their energy, impatiently turning backward, and sometimes abandon, under color of virtue, many of their exercises, saying to themselves, 'This labor does not profit me.' All this they do, because they feel themselves deprived of mental consolation. Such a soul acts imperfectly, for she has not yet unwound the bandage of spiritual self-love, for, had she unwound it, she would see that in truth everything proceeds from Me, that no leaf of a tree falls to the ground without My providence, and that what I give and promise to My creatures I give and promise to them for their sanctification, which is the good and end for which I created them." (CS, p. ?)

God the Father spoke to Catherine regarding why He takes worldly goods away from the just in order to increase their merit: "The righteous man is able to endure privation, and I take from him the goods of the world that he may the more abundantly enjoy the goods of Heaven." (CS, 175)

Jesus said to Saint Bridget of Sweden: "Just as a kingdom has sometimes been saved because of the charity of one human being, so some kingdoms have been lost because of one person's new inventions and burdensome vices. I give you an example of this in the case of the following kingdom: Its king trusted in money—exacted by fraud or feigned justice from his people and from travelers—more than he trusted in Me. Therefore, he lost his life and left his kingdom in trouble. Others who succeeded him turned his crooked inventions into custom, and, as it were, into law. But if a king trusts in Me, his God, and the community of the realm is petitioned for assistance with charity, then I am able to save and to restore to peace more quickly because of that charity. Therefore, if the king desires to prosper, let him keep his promise to Me and keep truth with the community of his realm; and let him especially beware of introducing new inventions or tributes or technicalities. In his difficulties, let him follow the advice of those who fear God, and not the advice of the covetous, for it is better to suffer some adversity in this world than to sin knowingly against Me and against his own soul." (BS, 86–87)

Jesus said to Bridget: "I, God, am Spirit. I speak and it is done. I instruct and all things obey Me. Truly I am He who gives existence and life to all. Before I made the sky and the mountains and the earth, in Myself I AM. I am above all and beyond all. I am within all, and all are in Me, and without Me there is nothing." (BS, 122)

God the Father said to Bridget: "Just as My works are many, so too they are wonderful and incomprehensible. And, many though they are, none are without cause. Man, indeed, is like a boy nurtured in a prison, in darkness. If one were to tell him that light and stars exist, he would not believe because he has never seen. Similarly, ever since man deserted the true light, he delights only in evil; evil seems sweet." (BS, 144)

Jesus said to Bridget: "It is therefore a token of great love that the prayers of My friends are not always heard—for the sake of their greater merit and for the proving of their constancy. For just as the Devil tries, if possible, to spoil the life of the just through some sin or through a contemptible death in order that the constancy of the faithful may thus grow tepid, so too I permit, not without cause, the testing of the just in order that their stability may be known to others and that they themselves may be more sublimely crowned." (BS, 145)

Mary said to Bridget: "Some [people's prayers] I answer by means of divine outpourings. To others, however, I speak more secretly, as is well pleasing to God." (BS, 206)

Regarding why He remains hidden from us, Jesus said to Bridget five days before she died: "I have done to you [during your life] what a bridegroom usually does, concealing himself from his bride so that he may be more diligently desired by her." (BS, 217)

Jesus said to Bridget: "Do not fear, but persist steadfastly in faith!" (BS, 153)

Jesus said to Bridget: "As to why I, the Son of God, said that I was ignorant of the hour of Judgment, I answer: It is written that Jesus advanced in age and wisdom. Everything that waxes and wanes has mutability; but the Godhead is immutable. Therefore, the fact that I, God's Son, co-eternal with the Father, advanced was the result of My human nature. What I did not know was what My humanity did not know. In My Godhead, I knew and know all things, for the Father does nothing other than the things that I, the Son, do." (BS, 149)

God

God the Father said to Saint Catherine of Siena: "Man is placed above all creatures and not beneath them. He cannot be satisfied or content except in something greater than himself. There is nothing greater than himself but Myself, the Eternal God." (CS, 203)

God the Father said to Catherine: "When [Jesus] ascended on high and returned to Me, the Father, I sent the Master, that is the Holy Spirit. He came to you with My power and the wisdom of My Son, and with His own peace and mercy, which is the essence of the Holy Spirit. He is one being with Me, the Father, and with My Son." (CS, 86)

God the Father told Catherine: "My power is not weakened, and cannot become weak." (CS, 101–102)

God the Father revealed to Catherine regarding humans: "I, being invisible, am not able to be seen by you until you become separated from your bodies. Then, indeed, you will see me, your God, and My Son, the Word, face to face. From now until after the general resurrection when your humanity will be conformed with the humanity of the Eternal Word, you can see Me with the eye of the intellect alone." (CS, 149)

God the Father said to Saint Bridget of Sweden: "If My glory were to be seen as it is, then man's perishable body would weaken and fail as did the senses of those who saw My glory on the mountain." (BS, 113)

God the Father said to Bridget: "Because there is no entrance into Heaven without the labor of charity, and so that faith may have its reward and the body may be capable of work, My glory is hidden for a time in order that, through desire and faith, it may be seen all the more fully and happily forever." (BS, 113)

God the Father said to Bridget: "In My Godhead all that is going to exist or happen is foreseen and foreknown from the beginning as if it had already occurred. The fall of man was foreknown, and out of God's justice it was permitted, but it was not caused by God and did not have to happen because of God's foreknowledge. Foreknown too from eternity was man's liberation, which was to happen out of God's mercy." (BS, 116)

God the Father said to Bridget: "If any human's body were to see the Godhead, it would melt like wax before a fire, and the soul would rejoice with such great exultation that the body would be annihilated like a cinder." (BS, 125)

God the Father said to Bridget: "Not even the prophets saw Me as I am in the nature of My Godhead; for even those who heard the voice of My Godhead and saw the smoking mountain were terrified and said, 'Let Moses speak to us, and we shall hear him.' Therefore, in order that man might better understand Me, I, God the merciful, showed Myself to him in a form like himself that could be seen and touched—namely, in My humanity, in which the Godhead exists but, as it were, veiled—in order that man might not be terrified by a form unlike himself. For, insofar as I am God, I am not corporeal and not corporeally portrayed; therefore, it was in My humanity that I could be heard and seen more tolerably by man." (BS, 125)

While she was in the city of Ortona in the kingdom of Naples, Jesus spoke to Bridget regarding the "treasure" of God's grace—the gift of God's love. Bridget was "wide awake and at prayer" when her heart began to burn so profusely that it seemed her heart was on fire with God's love. She became "entirely full of spiritual joy" to such a degree that her body, she thought, might fail in its strength and she would not be able to endure. Then she heard a voice that said to her: "I am the Creator and Redeemer of all. Know therefore that such a joy as you now feel in your soul is a treasure of Mine." (BS, 162)

God the Father said to Bridget: "With me, the good and the wicked cannot dwell together at one time any more than light can dwell together with darkness." (BS, 149)

Jesus told Bridget to go to Rome, but she resisted, pleading her age and weakness. Jesus said: "Why do you plead your age? I am the Creator of nature; I can weaken or strengthen nature as it pleases Me. I will be with you. I will direct your way. I will guide you and lead you back." (BS, 171)

Grace

God the Father said to Saint Catherine of Siena: "He who loves Me more receives more. Your reward is measured according to the measure of your love." (CS, 262)

God the Father said to Catherine: "I wish you to know, My daughter, that I have recreated and restored to the life of grace the human race through the Blood of My only-begotten Son. Yet, men are not grateful, but go from bad to worse and from guilt to guilt, even persecuting Me with many injuries and taking so little account of the graces which I have given and continue to give them. Not only do they not attribute what they have received to grace, but [believe] on occasion to receive injuries from Me, as if I would desire anything other than their sanctification." (CS, 70–71)

God the Father said to Catherine: "It is right that he who receives more should render more, and should be under great obligations to Him from whom he receives more." (CS, 70–71)

God the Father said to Catherine: "I have already told you that the delights of the world, without Me, are venomous thorns. The vision of the intellect is deluded by them. The affection of the will is deluded into loving them, and the memory into retaining remembrance of them. The unity of these powers of the soul is so great that I cannot be offended by one without all the others offending Me at the same time. The one presents to the other, as I told you, good or evil, according to the pleasure of the free will. This free will is bound to the affection, and it moves as it pleases, either with the light of reason or without it. Your reason is attached to Me when your will does not cut it off from Me by misdirected love." (CS, 132)

God the Father said to Catherine: "The only thing you possess is the affection and desire of your souls." (CS, 198)

Saint Bridget of Sweden heard in spirit: "Say to the bishop, 'I am He who filled the shepherd with My Spirit. Was this because of the shepherd's fasting? I am He who made married men prophets. What had they done to merit this? I commanded a prophet to take an adulteress as his wife. Did he not obey? I am He who spoke as well to Job in his delights as when he sat upon the dunghill. Therefore, because I am wonderful, I do all things that please Me without dependence on preceding merits.'" (BS, 88)

God the Father said to Bridget: "Because it was not fitting for Me to have any diminishment in My hosts [i.e. angels], I therefore created, in place of those who fell, another creature—namely, man—who, through his free choice and his good will, might merit the same dignity that the [fallen] angels deserted." (BS, 117)

Jesus said to Bridget: "When you people entered My temple, which was dedicated with My Blood, you were as cleansed of all your sins as if you had at that moment been lifted from the font of Baptism. And because of your labors and devotion, some souls of your relatives that were in Purgatory have this day been liberated and have entered into Heaven in My glory. For all who come to this place with a perfect will to amend their lives in accord with their better conscience, and who are not willing to fall back into their former sins, will have all their former sins completely forgiven; and they will have an increase of grace to make progress." (BS, 187–188)

Jesus said to Bridget: "Although My grace has been withdrawn from many in their ingratitude, nevertheless others will come who will arise in lieu of them and who will obtain My grace." (BS, 217–218)

Jesus said to Bridget: "Go to Rome, where the streets are paved with gold and reddened with the blood of saints and where there is a compendium—i.e. a shorter way—to Heaven because of the indulgences that the holy pontiffs have merited by their prayers." (BS, 92)

God the Father said to Bridget: "Because many are ungrateful for My grace and become more undevout the more their gifts are multiplied, the gifts are therefore quickly taken from them in order that My divine plan may be more swiftly manifested and lest man abuse My grace to his own greater doom." (BS, 134)

God the Father said to Bridget: "[The Holy Spirit] ascends [in power and glory] when He elevates the mind through subtlety of understanding and through devotion of soul and through the inflaming of spiritual desire. He descends when He permits the mind to be perturbed by tribulations . . ." (BS, 150)

Jesus said to Bridget: "The kingdom [of Sweden] is entangled in a great and long-unpunished sin. Therefore My words cannot yet rise and bear fruit here." (BS, 153–154)

Saint Botvid said to Bridget: "I have, with other saints, merited for you God's grace—namely, to hear and to see and to feel spiritual things—and the Spirit of God will inflame your soul." (BS, 78)

Saint Margaret of Cortona feared that she was being deluded by the deceiver of souls with all the extraordinary graces she received. She felt herself unworthy of divine revelation and exclaimed: "O enemy of souls if it is you who are speaking to me, transforming yourself into an angel of light, I command you in Christ's name be silent and depart."

Jesus said, "I, Jesus, your Redeemer, whom you love and seek above all things, I tell you that you are My beloved child to whom such gifts have been given as have not been given to any woman upon the earth."

Margaret then humbly asked why she was deserving of such gifts, especially since she was one so weak in body, unable to do great things for God.

Jesus replied, "My child Margaret, do you not desire Me above all things? Would you not willingly die for Me? Are you not poor for love of Me? Is your life not just one continuous desire for Me and Me alone? And do you not walk constantly in fear lest in any action you should at all offend Me?

When Margaret admitted all this was true, Jesus said, "In these ways, daughter, you deserve Me and win for yourself My favors. Therefore, love Me as I love you. Give praise to Me, for I will praise you and cause all the world to praise you." (MC, 135–36)

One day, Jesus spoke to Margaret about His efforts to draw men to Himself: "O incredulous one! How little do you know what I have done in these saints, and how I have inclined Myself to them that they might come to Me. How little do you know of My condescension to many who still live upon the earth! Would you have the door of My mercy closed against you, that you do speak thus? But the vision of My immensity and loveliness is your excuse. I tell you if all the purity of the angels in Heaven and of the saints, whether in Heaven or upon earth, were brought together, it still would be but as darkness before the sun of My spotless purity were I not to incline Myself to them. My child, did I not descend from Heaven to earth and take the flesh of the Virgin Mary? Yes, O My simple one, and I thus came down to earth that sinners might touch Me and I be a sojourner in their midst and eat with them." (MC, 169–171)

Saint Margaret of Cortona once spoke to Jesus, saying: "Truly you are my Father, my Awakener, my Spouse, my Gladness, Joy of all joys!"

Jesus replied, "And you are My child, My companion, My chosen one."

Margaret then said, "Lord, don't send me back into the desert [the desert of the world, which is deprived of the glory of God]."

Jesus said, "I send you back even as a sheep among wolves."

Margaret, after some consideration, said, "My Lord, let this citadel of my body be quickly destroyed so that through the ruins I may pass to You."

Jesus replied, "And yet no suffering is so bitter to you as to be without Me."

Margaret answered, "You are indeed, Lord, my very life, through Whom I live. If You send me back into the desert I shall die. You are my treasure; without You all wealth is to me but direst poverty."

Jesus repeated again that Margaret had to go back into the desert. But while saying this, He smiled lovingly and showed Himself to her. Margaret saw Him in her mind's eye seated upon a majestic throne. To His right, seated upon a throne of indescribable magnificence, was Jesus' Virgin Mother, Mary. She was situated far above the angels and she greeted Margaret, wishing her profound joy.

Jesus then went further and invited her to view an awe-inspiring vision of all the assembled blessed in Heaven. Showered with all these special favors, Margaret was overwhelmed with joy, and she almost burst with happiness to the point that she could barely say, "O my Lord, Whom alone I love, for You have created me only for You, my desire is to see You Who have filled me with such joy that I can neither be silent nor speak."

Turning again to Mary, Margaret asked, "Lady, speak for me, I beg you, that your Son might show me the joy of His face."

Jesus immediately heard her prayer. Even though He had earlier refused her, He then showed Himself to Margaret, at the same time telling her again that she must go back into the desert. Margaret protested, "Lord, that will be a pain most hard to bear."

But Jesus replied, "My child, remember what I told you in the beginning when I came to you, how you would be fed on the Cross." (MC, 222–224)

Hell

Regarding the state of souls in Hell, God the Father told Saint Catherine of Siena: "My daughter, the tongue is not sufficient to narrate the pain of these poor souls." (CS, 105)

God the Father said to Saint Bridget of Sweden: "If Hell pains were visibly seen as they now exist, man would be totally frozen with fear and would seek Heaven out of fear and not out of love. Since no one ought to seek Heavenly joy out of fear of punishment but rather out of divine charity, these pains are therefore now hidden." (BS, 114)

God the Father said to Catherine: "A false Christian is punished [in Hell] more than a pagan, and the deathless fire of divine justice consumes him more. . . . [In Hell] they ask for death and cannot have it, for they cannot lose their being. . . . Guilt is more gravely punished [in Hell] after the redemption of the Blood than before, because man received more. But sinners seem neither to understand this nor to pay any attention to their own sins and so become My enemies, even though I have reconciled them by means of the Blood of my Son." (CS, 72)

God the Father said to Catherine: "In Hell, the souls have four principal torments out of which proceed all the other torments. The first is that they see themselves deprived of the vision of Me, which is such pain to them that were it possible, they would rather choose the fire and the tortures and torments and to see Me, rather than be without the torments and not to see Me. . . .The second [is] the worm of conscience, which gnaws unceasingly, seeing that the soul is deprived of Me and of the conversation of the angels. Through her sin [she is] made worthy, rather, of conversation with—and the sight of—the devils. The vision of the Devil is the third pain and redoubles every toil for them . . . because in seeing him they know themselves more, that is to say, that they know that by their own sin they have made themselves worthy of [the Devil]. The fourth torment they have is the fire. This fire burns yet does not consume. The being of the soul cannot be consumed, because it is not a material thing that fire can consume." (CS, 105–106)

Holiness

God the Father said to Saint Catherine of Siena: "I want you to know that every virtue is obtained through your neighbor. The same is true with every defect. So whoever hates Me does an injury to his neighbor and to himself. He who stands in hatred of Me does an injury to his neighbor and to himself. . . . You are obliged to love your neighbor as yourself. In loving him, you need to help him spiritually—with prayer, counsel and giving him both spiritual and temporal assistance according to his need. A man who does not love, does not help [his neighbor]. So he gives himself an injury: he cuts off grace from himself and injures his neighbor by depriving him of the benefit of prayers." (CS, 39–40)

God the Father said to Catherine: "Now I wish to tell you further, that a man proves his patience with his neighbor when he receives injuries from him. Similarly, he proves his humility with a proud man, his faith with an infidel, his true hope with one who despairs, his justice with the unjust, his kindness with the cruel, his gentleness and his long-suffering with the irascible. Good men produce and prove all their virtues [by how they deal with] their neighbor, just as perverse men [prove] all their vices [by the same way]." (CS, 48)

God the Father said to Catherine: "I take delight in few words and many [good] works." (CS, 55)

God the Father said to Saint Catherine of Siena: "I want to show you how [people] deceive themselves, and how, wishing to flee troubles, they still fall into them. Since it seems to some that following Me—that is, walking by the way of the bridge, the Word, My Son—is great toil—they draw back, fearing the hardship. This is because they are blinded and do not know or see the Truth, as you know. . . . Conscience always fights on one side, and sensuality on the other; but as soon as he, with hatred and displeasure of himself, manfully makes up his mind, saying, 'I wish to follow Christ crucified,' he breaks at once the deceit, and finds inestimable sweetness . . . some finding more and some less, according to their disposition and desire." (CS, 122–123)

Regarding sin and imperfect love, God the Father said to Catherine: "It is not enough for eternal life to flee sin from fear of punishment, or to embrace virtue from the motive of one's own advantage. Sin should be abandoned because it is displeasing to Me, and virtue should be loved for My sake. Every person is first called in this way. But this is because the soul herself is at first imperfect. She must advance from imperfection to perfection, either while she lives by a generous love to Me with a pure and virtuous heart that takes no thought for herself, or at least in the moment of death, recognizing her own imperfection . . . It was with this imperfect love that Saint Peter loved the sweet and good Jesus, My only-begotten Son, enjoying most pleasantly His sweet conversation. But when the time of trouble came, he failed. So disgraceful was his fall, that not only could he not bear any pain himself, but his terror of the very approach of pain caused him to fall and deny the Lord with the words: 'I have never known Him.'" (CS, 144–145)

Catherine devotion to Jesus was so strong and unwavering that her penances and fasts were beyond what an ordinary human would ever dare to undertake. Nevertheless, she was determined to prove her love for Jesus and to never abstain from any sacrifice that she believed would bring either her soul or another's closer to God. One year, on the day before the beginning of Lent—described in her day as "the vain feast of the stomach" because of the gluttonous eating that took place—Catherine was alone in her room fasting and seeking God with all her heart. Suddenly, Jesus appeared to her and said: "Since for love of Me you have forsaken vanities and despised the pleasure of the flesh and fastened all delights of your heart on Me, now, when the rest of the household are feasting and enjoying themselves, I have determined to celebrate the wedding feast of your soul and to espouse you to Me in faith as I promised." *Before He was finished speaking, five other souls appeared there as well: the Virgin Mary, the apostles John and Paul, Saint Dominic and the prophet David. As music poured forth from the instrument in David's hands, Mary took Catherine's hand in hers and presented her to Jesus, asking Him to marry her. Jesus graciously agreed, and produced a spectacular golden ring studded with four pearls set in a circle. In the center of the ring was placed a diamond of incomparable beauty. With His right hand He slipped the ring onto Catherine's second finger, saying solemnly,* "I marry you to Me in faith, to Me, your creator and savior. Keep this faith unspotted until you come to Me in Heaven and celebrate the marriage that has no end." (CS, ?)

God the Father said to Catherine: "In as much as desire is never ended, it is never satisfied in this life, but the more the soul loves, the less she seems to herself to love." (CS, 197)

God the Father said to Catherine: "Virtue cannot be proved except by its contrary. Sensuality is contrary to the spirit, and yet, by means of [the denial of] sensuality, the soul is able to prove the love which she has for Me, her creator." (CS, 208)

While God the Father spoke to Catherine about the death of a just soul—"at the moment of death she realizes better the value of time and the jewels of virtue"—*He went on to say that such a soul does not grow proud in these past virtuous acts, but still places all trust in the mercy of God:* "The just man does not turn his head to admire his past virtues, because he neither can nor will hope in his own virtues, but only in the Blood [of Jesus] in which he has found mercy. And as he lived in the memory of that Blood, so in death he is inebriated and drowned in the same." (CS, 260)

Regarding the imperfect souls who wish to choose their mortifications rather than simply accept what God sends them, the Lord said to Catherine: "[They cheat] themselves with the delusion of their own self-will: 'I wish to have that consolation, and not these battles or these temptations of the Devil, not indeed, for my own pleasure, but in order to please God the more and in order to retain Him the more in my soul through grace—because it seems to me that I should possess Him more and serve Him better in that way than in this.' And this is the way the soul often falls into trouble and becomes tedious and insupportable to herself, thus injuring her own perfection. . . . Now, if the soul were not in this condition, but were truly humble and not presumptuous, she would be illuminated to see that I [God] grant condition and time and place and consolations and tribulations as they may be needed for your salvation, and to complete the perfection to which I have elected the soul." (CS, ?)

God the Father spoke to Catherine about those souls who have achieved a high state of perfection and how they accept with love both trials and consolations: "These deem themselves worthy of the troubles and stumbling-blocks caused them by the world, and of the privation of their own consolation, and indeed of whatever circumstance happens to them. And inasmuch as they deem themselves worthy of trouble, so also do they deem themselves unworthy of the fruit which they receive after their trouble. They have known and tasted in the light My eternal will, which wishes for nothing else but your good, and gives and permits these troubles in order that you should be sanctified in Me." (CS, 213)

God the Father spoke to Catherine about perfectly converted souls and their desire to serve simply out of love rather than any recompense or reward: "She does not see herself in herself, seeking her own consolation either in spiritual or temporal [things], but like one who has placed his all in this light and knowledge, and has destroyed his own will, she shuns no labor from whatever source it comes, but rather, enduring the troubles, the insults, the temptations of the Devil, and the murmurings of men, eats at the table of the most holy cross. . . . Seeking no reward either from Me or from creatures—because she is stripped of mercenary love, that is, of love for Me based on [selfish] motives—[she] is clothed in perfect light, loving Me in perfect purity with no other regard than for the praise and glory of My name, serving neither Me for her own delight nor her neighbor for her own profit, but purely through love alone." (CS, 215)

God the Father said to Catherine: "I am that fire which purifies the soul, and the closer the soul is to Me, the purer she becomes, and the further she is from Me, the more does her purity leave her." (CS, 218)

God the Father told Catherine: "Oh, best loved and dearest daughter! I will fulfill your desire in this request [to continue to converse and learn more about God], in order that, on your side, you may not sin through ignorance or negligence, for a fault of yours would be more serious and worthy of graver reproof now than before, because you have learned more of My truth." (CS, 226)

Jesus spoke to Catherine regarding the great dignity of man in the following words: "You have greater dignity and excellence than the angels, for I took your human nature and not that of the angels. Therefore, as I have said to you, I, God, have become man, and man has become God by the union of My divine nature with your human nature." (CS, 228)

Regarding souls, particularly those in religious orders, who do not keep watch over their passions, God the Father said: "It is impossible for a man with many worldly relations, of delicate habits and disordinate greediness, who is not watchful of himself or prays, to keep his mind pure." *God the Father continued, saying that, in contrast to the souls that are not watchful over their passions, those who strive for holiness will embrace poverty over riches:* "He has abandoned his temporal substance, observing so perfectly the vow of poverty, that he blames himself for considering even the necessities of his body. His cell is full of the odor of poverty and not of clothes, he has no fear that thieves will come to rob him or that rust or moths will corrupt his garments, and if anything is given to him, he does not think of laying it by for his own use, but freely shares it with his brothers, not thinking of tomorrow, but rather depriving himself today of what he needs, thinking only of the kingdom of Heaven and how he may best observe true obedience. And in order that he may better keep to the path of humility, he submits to small and great, to poor and rich, and becomes the servant of all, never refusing labor, but serving all with charity." (CS, 304, 309–301)

Jesus gave to Saint Bridget of Sweden a message for Lord Bernard, Neapolitan archbishop: "Say also to the parish priests that they are to correct their parishioners and to rebuke them for their open sins in cases that pertain to them in order that they may be able to live better lives. Those parishioners who are unwilling to be rebuked [by the priests] should then be rebuked by you. . . . Nor are you bound to forego rebukes out of fear for your body unless, by chance, some danger to souls should come from them." (BS, 180)

Regarding her being drawn away from worldly pleasures, Jesus said to Bridget: "From these things you were drawn away, and you were led into the mansion of the Holy Spirit. He is in Me, and I am in Him, and He encloses you in Himself. He, indeed, is most pure and most beautiful and most steadfast, for He sustains all things. Therefore, conform yourself to the Inhabitant of the house by remaining pure, humble, and devout." (BS, 139)

God the Father said to Bridget: "The abundance of one's wisdom does not profit the soul's eternal salvation unless the soul also shines with a good life. On the contrary, it is more useful to have less knowledge and a better life. Therefore, each person has been given a measure of rationality by means of which he can obtain Heaven if he lives piously." (BS, 136)

Jesus said to Bridget regarding the queen of Cyprus: "She should nurture her son with divine charity and appoint as his councilors men who are just and not covetous, and as members of his household men who are modest, composed and wise. From these he may learn to fear God, to rule justly, to sympathize with the unfortunate, to flee from flatterers and sycophants like poison and to seek the advice of just men, even if they are poor, lowly or despised." (BS, 193)

One day after she had received Holy Communion, Jesus spoke to Saint Margaret of Cortona: "My child, however hard your own sufferings may be, do not cease from trying to root out vice from the heart of the sinner and to plant in him the seed of virtue. Scatter the good seed, and I will [also] give you seed to scatter, because I will put the saving word of grace into your mouth. And even though I might stop conversing with you, I will still continue to enlighten you so that your words may be true." (MC, 263)

Hope

God the Father said to Saint Catherine of Siena: "With the same measure that My creatures hope in Me will My providence be measured to them." (CS, 250)

God the Father spoke to Catherine about souls that lose hope in God's mercy: "Despair is that sin which is pardoned neither here nor hereafter. It is because despair displeases Me so much that I wish them to hope in My mercy at the point of death, even if their life has been disordered and wicked." (CS, 267–268)

Jesus said to Saint Bridget of Sweden: "My words—which you hear from Me frequently in spiritual vision—like the good drink, satisfy those who thirst for true charity; second, they warm those who are cold; third, they gladden those who are disturbed; and fourth, they heal those who are weak in soul." (BS, 148)

An angel said to Bridget: "It is entirely certain that all who preserve themselves from Hell by truly repenting their sins, by voluntarily conforming themselves to the divine will, and by loving God Himself with all their hearts, will obtain His grace." (BS, 186)

Humility

God the Father said to Saint Catherine of Siena: "No virtue, daughter, can have life in itself except through charity and humility, which is the foster mother and nurse of charity." (CS, 32)

God the Father said to Saint Catherine of Siena: "In knowledge of self you will humble yourself, seeing that in yourself you do not even exist. For your very being, as you will learn, is derived from Me, since I have loved both you and others before you were in existence." (CS, 32–33)

Jesus said to Saint Bridget of Sweden: "If I had come [to earth] with great power and honor, how then would the proud have been humbled? Or will the proud now enter Heaven? Not at all! And so I came humbly [in a manger] in order that man might learn humility." (BS, 130)

Jesus spoke to Bridget about a duke who was proud and frequently boasted: "This man boldly expands his pride. He boasts of his incontinence and is not attentive to the things that he has done to his neighbor. Therefore, if he does not humble himself, I will act in accord with the common proverb: 'No lighter wails he who afterward weeps than he who wailed before.' For he shall have a death no lighter than his brother's—no, a death more bitter—unless he quickly amends himself." (BS, 191)

Parents began to hold such a reverence for Saint Margaret of Cortona that they would beg her to hold their children at the baptismal font. She began to refuse the requests, fearing she would be honored. She was then begged by the wife of a Syndic [friend of the friars], for whom she held great respect, to assist at the Baptism of her infant son. After assisting at the Baptism, Jesus commanded her not to assist with Baptisms again or even leave her house at all. He said to her: "My child, three signs of grace I have given you, which the world may see: in the first place, you have a greater fear of Me than most people have; secondly you are utterly ashamed of your sins; and thirdly, you are humble in spite of the esteem in which others regard you." (MC, 128–129)

Once a boy was troubled by an evil spirit. Each time the boy was conjured to reveal by whose intercession he might be delivered, he responded, "By the prayers and merits of sister Margaret who lives in Cortona." *The evil spirit, unable to bear even the atmosphere sanctified by the prayers of Margaret, left the boy, crying aloud,* "I give back the boy; take him home again, for I will not be led into Cortona into the presence of that Margaret, whose prayers are as fire to us."

Out of gratitude someone brought the saved boy to Margaret to thank her, which then sent Margaret into great grief. She believed that God alone should be thanked for the deliverance. The people, however, were consoled and had no doubt that the miracle [of the boy's healing] was through Margaret's intercession.

On another occasion Margaret was conversing with Jesus on the second Sunday of Advent. She asked Him: "My Lord, what shall I do in order to live to the end in You? Because of the [special intimacy I have enjoyed with You], I have become too familiar, and [now] do not respect Your greatness with a proper fear, and I do not keep in mind my own lowliness."

Jesus answered her: "My child, keep a pure mind. Your prayer was pleasing to Me when you prayed that you might be subject to all creatures. So I command you from now on to subject yourself not only to Me, but to all creatures in so far as it will be to My glory. For love of Me, hold yourself contemptible in the sight of all mankind, imitating My example, for I made Myself subject to all men, and willed that they should hold Me in contempt.

"This humble lowering of yourself will exalt you among the blessed who are in Heaven. Be white in your innocence and ruddy in your love, because you are the third light granted to the Order of My beloved Francis. He is the first light, shining in the Order of the Friars Minor. The Blessed Clare is the second light, shining in the order of the nuns. And you are the third light, in the order of the Penitents." (MC, 287–288)

Jesus

God the Father said to Saint Catherine of Siena: "You will see how those handle themselves who walk in the light, as well as those who walk in the darkness. I also wish you to look at the bridge of My only-begotten Son. See how great it is, because it reaches from Heaven to earth. By means of this bridge, the earth of your humanity is joined to the greatness of the Deity. I say then that this bridge reaches from Heaven to earth, and constitutes the union which I have made with man. . . . Please take note that it is not simply enough that in order to have life My Son made this bridge for you; you must also walk on it." (CS, 75–76)

The Virgin Mary said: "There is the same humility in my Son now in the power of His Godhead as there was then, when He was laid in the manger. Although He knew all things in accordance with His Godhead, nevertheless, while lying between two animals, He spoke nothing at all, in accordance with His humanity. So too now, sitting at the right hand of the Father, He hears all who speak to Him with love, and He answers through infusions of the Holy Spirit. To some He speaks with words and thoughts, to others as if from mouth to mouth, just as it pleases Him." (BS, 206)

The Virgin Mary said to Saint Bridget of Sweden: "I, indeed, who gave birth to the true God Himself, bear witness to the fact that the same Jesus Christ, my Son, had one personal possession and that He alone possessed it. This was that tunic that I made with my own hands." (BS, 170)

Judgment

God the Father said to Saint Catherine of Siena: "I give My servants a hunger and a desire for My honor and the salvation of souls. This is so that, being held back by their tears, I may mitigate the fury of My divine justice." (CS, 72)

God the Father said to Catherine: "The soul will return with the body, [both] in the just to be glorified and in the damned to be tortured eternally. . . . My Truth and all the blessed ones will reproach [the damned] greatly and make them ashamed. The worm of conscience will gnaw the pith of the tree, that is, the soul, and also the bark outside, which is the body. They will be reproached for the Blood that was shed for them, and by the works of mercy, spiritual and temporal, which I did for them by means of My Son, and which they should have done for their neighbor, as is contained in the Holy Gospel." (CS, 115)

God the Father spoke to Catherine about the state of the unrepentant sinner after death: "Not so excellent, dearest daughter, is the end of these other poor wretches who are in great misery. How terrible and dark is their death! At the moment of death, the Devil accuses them with great terror and darkness, showing his face, which you know is so horrible that the creature would rather choose any pain that can be suffered in this world than see it. So greatly does he freshen the sting of conscience that it gnaws him horribly. He made inordinate delights and sensuality to be lords over his reason. These [sins] accuse him miserably, because then he knows the truth of that which at first he did not know, and his errors bring him great confusion." (CS, 265)

God the Father spoke to Catherine about Judgment Day and how souls will perceive Jesus: "He will not come thus [as a baby in a manger], but He will come with power to reprove in His own person, and will render to everyone his due. . . . There will be no one on that day who will not tremble. To the miserable ones who are damned, [Jesus'] aspect will cause such torment and terror that the tongue cannot describe it. To the just it will cause the fear of reverence with great joy—not because His face changes, because He is unchangeable. . . .

The condemned [will] see His countenance in darkness, in confusion and in hatred." (CS, 108)

God the Father said to Catherine: "The hatred [of the damned] is so great that they cannot will or desire any good . . . [once] the life of man ends, free-will is bound. Therefore they cannot merit, having lost, as they have, the time to do so. If they finish their life dying in hatred with the guilt of mortal sin, their souls, by divine justice, remain forever bound with the bonds of hatred . . . especially the pains of those who have been the cause of damnation to others." (CS, 108–109)

God the Father spoke about the souls of the blessed in the afterlife: "They cannot do any meritorious act by which they could merit anything, because in this life alone can they merit and sin, according to their free will. These, then, do not await with fear but with joy the divine judgment, and the face of My Son will not seem to them terrible or full of hatred, because they finished their lives in love and affection for Me and [with] good will toward their neighbor. So you see then that the transformation is not in His face, when He comes to judge with My Divine Majesty, but in the vision of those who will be judged by Him. To the damned He will appear with hatred and with justice, but to the saved with love and mercy." (CS, 114)

God the Father said: "At the time of death, the soul only is reproved, but at the General Judgment the soul is reproved together with the body, because the body has been the companion and instrument of the soul—to do good or evil according to one's free will. Every work, good or bad, is done by means of the body. Therefore, My daughter, glory and infinite good are rendered to My elect ones with their glorified body, rewarding them for the toils they bore for Me together with the soul. But to the perverse ones will be rendered eternal pains by means of their body, because their body was the instrument of evil." (CS, 114)

God the Father said to Catherine: "To the just man [at the Final Judgment], the appearance and vision of the Devil causes no harm or fear, for fear and harm can only be caused to him by sin. Those who have passed their lives lasciviously and in many sins receive both harm and fear from the appearance of the Devils. They don't receive the harm of despair if they do not wish it, but they do receive the suffering of condemnation, of the refreshing of the worm of conscience, and of fear and terror at their horrible appearance. See now, dearest daughter, how different are the sufferings and the battle of death to a just man and to a sinner, and how different is their end." (CS, 271–272)

Regarding the souls of the just who enter the afterlife with the love of God in their hearts, God the Father told Catherine: "The just soul for whom life finishes in the affection of charity and bonds of love cannot increase in virtue, time having ended, but she can always love with that affection with which she comes to Me. . . . With that measure of love with which they have come to Me, [so] is it measured to them. . . . And they rejoice and exult with the angels with whom they are placed, according to their various and unique virtues [that they practiced] in the world, being all bound in the bonds of love. And they have a special participation with those whom they closely loved with particular affection in the world."(CS, p. ?)

Justice

God the Father said to Saint Bridget of Sweden: "Friend, I am God the Creator of all. I do not act less justly to the wicked than to the good, for I am justice itself. My justice decrees that entrance into Heaven must be obtained through steadfast faith and rational hope and fervent charity." (BS, 112)

Jesus said to Bridget: "I, God, who alone am just, came to justify all." (BS, 131)

God the Father said to Bridget: "Because man is more worthy and more noble than all creatures, man ought to live more nobly than all, for he, in preference to others, has been enriched with reason. But if many abuse reason and My divine gifts, what wonder is it if, at the time of justice, I punish that which was passed over in the time of mercy?" (BS, p. 152)

Jesus spoke to Bridget regarding a monk who was considered arrogant and less than diligent in his vocation: "Oh, how happy you would be if you had paid attention to your profession and your vow!" (BS, 152)

Regarding a certain nobleman who was an administrator and a senator, Mary said to Bridget: "Advise him to do justice wherever he can. If he knows that he has goods that were wrongly acquired, he must not delay in making restitution. He must also be careful not to impose unusual burdens on his subjects, and he must be content with the things that he has because they are sufficient for him if he manages them discreetly and with moderation. Women other than his own wife he must avoid like poison, and he must not lead out the army against anyone or take part in the action himself unless he fully knows that justice is on his side and that the war is just. He must also be zealous in making frequent use of confession and in receiving the Body of Christ more frequently and in occupying himself, at fixed times in the day, with the remembrance of Christ's passion and his wounds." (BS, 176)

Love

God the Father said to Saint Catherine of Siena: "Through the ineffable love I have for you, wishing to [re-introduce] you to grace, I have washed you and recreated you in the Blood of My only-begotten Son, spilled with so great a fire of love." (CS, 33)

God the Father told Catherine: "Open the eye of your intellect and gaze into Me, and you will see the beauty of My rational creatures. And among the beauties which I have given to the soul, creating her in My image and likeness, look at those creatures who are clothed with the wedding garment (the garment of love) adorned with many virtues by which they are united with Me through love." (CS, 27)

God the Father told Catherine: "To him who will love Me and will observe My commandment, will I manifest Myself: and he shall be one thing with Me and I with him." (CS, 27)

God the Father told Catherine: "The Apostle Paul wrote: 'If I had the tongues of angels, and if I knew the things of the future and gave my body to be burned, and have not love, it would be worth nothing to me.'" *He then added:* "The glorious Apostle thus shows that finite works are not valid, either as punishment or recompense, without the condiment of the affection of love." (CS, 31)

God the Father said to Catherine: "Charity gives life to all the virtues; no virtue can be obtained without charity." (CS, 44)

God the Father said to Catherine: "This is Saint Paul's counsel to you when he says that charity ought to be concerned first with self. Otherwise, it will never be of perfect use to others. When perfection is not in the soul, everything which the soul does for itself and for others is imperfect." (CS, 59)

God the Father said to Catherine: "It now remains to be told to you how it can be seen that souls have arrived at perfect love. This is seen by the same sign that was given to the holy disciples after they had received the Holy Spirit, when they came forth from the house and fearlessly announced the doctrine of My Word, My only-begotten Son. They did not fear pain, but rather gloried in it. They did not mind going before the tyrants of the world to announce to them the truth for the glory and praise of My name." (CS, 169)

God the Father told Catherine: "Every perfection and every virtue proceeds from charity, and charity is nourished by humility, which results from the knowledge and holy hatred of self, that is, sensuality." (CS, 151)

God the Father said to Catherine: "The soul always fears until she arrives at true love." (CS, 151)

God the Father spoke to Catherine about how to recognize imperfect love: "Do you know how the imperfection of spiritual love for the creature is shown? It is shown when the lover feels pain if it appears to him that the object of his love does not satisfy or return his love, or when he sees the beloved one's conversation turned aside from him, or himself deprived of consolation, or another loved more than he. In these and in many other ways can it be seen that his neighborly love is still imperfect. . . . It is because his love for Me is still imperfect that his neighborly love is so weak and because the root of self-love has not been properly dug out." (CS, 156)

God the Father said to Catherine: "Charity is itself continual prayer." (CS, 167)

God the Father said to Catherine: "Every exercise, whether performed in one's self or in one's neighbor, with good will, is prayer." (CS, 167)

God the Father said to Catherine: "Unless the soul keeps to this path [of fervent prayer and self-denial], she will always remain tepid and imperfect, and will only love Me and her neighbor in proportion to the pleasure which she finds in My service." (CS, 167)

God the Father said to Catherine: "The heart grieves in proportion to the love it feels." (CS, 199)

Jesus appeared to Saint Bridget of Sweden while she was in Jerusalem, seated on a throne surrounded by saints: "I am supreme charity itself, for all things that I have done from eternity, I have done out of charity. In the same way, all things that I do and shall do in the future proceed entirely from My charity. For charity is as incomprehensible and intense in Me now as it was at the time of My Passion when, through My death and out of exceeding charity, I freed from [the abode of the dead] all the elect who were worthy of this redemption and liberation. For if it were still possible that I might die as many times as there are souls in [the abode of the dead] so that for each of them I might again endure such a death as I then endured for all, My body would still be ready to undergo all these things with a glad will and most perfect charity." (BS, 196–197)

God the Father said to Bridget: "That which is more fervently loved by the heart is more frequently thought of and more diligently adored." (BS, 112)

Saint Margaret of Cortona had been praying that God would favor her by showing her even greater marks of His love than He showed to every other man and woman in the world. While she was praying for this favor, Jesus said to her: "My child, you have not yet perfect charity, and in your present state you must walk in reverence even as in charity. And into your reverence there must enter a knowledge of yourself which will prevent you from ever asking anything for yourself with forwardness or elation of spirit.

"Perfect charity is found in the soul which by love is lifted up above itself and so passes onto Me that it prefers its fellow creatures to itself—like a man invited to a marriage feast. He would be one who allows others to take the most honorable places while he himself takes the lowest. He would be one who follows the others as they enter the king's palace and does not seek to go before them. Yet don't be upset because of this prayer of yours. Even as I forgave Peter when in an excess of love he cut off the ear of a man in the hour of My betrayal, so do I forgive you now." (MC, 231–232)

Love of God

God the Father said to Saint Catherine of Siena: "All evils spring from the soul's lack of love of Me and her neighbor. To the extent that a man does not do good, it follows that he must do evil. To whom does he do evil? Firstly, to himself and then to his neighbor—not against Me, for no evil can touch Me except . . . that which he does to himself." (CS, 40)

On more than one occasion Catherine was witnessed to have been transfigured during the Holy Sacrifice of the Mass. Blessed Raymond, her biographer, wrote that one particular morning while saying Mass in her presence he turned to give his blessing at the proper interval and "saw that her face had become like an angel's and was sending out bright rays of light." He wrote that her face shone with "brilliance" and that he was "absolutely dumbfounded" to witness such a marvel. On another occasion her first confessor, Fra Tommaso, was celebrating Mass and turned to offer Holy Communion to her. He then saw a marvel that left him dumbstruck: he saw her face "bathed in tears and sweat, but shining and as though on fire," and she received Holy Communion with such devotion that he marveled at her great devotion and holiness. The following day Fra Tommaso sought out Catherine "whom he had seen with such a burning face" and asked what had taken place. She replied that it was an extraordinary encounter with Jesus, concluding: "I wonder how ever I managed to go on living in such an excess of ardor and love."

God the Father said to Catherine of "I will manifest Myself to [souls], as My Truth said in these words: 'He who loves Me shall be one with Me and I with him, and I will manifest Myself to him and we will dwell together.' This is the state of two dear friends. For though they are two in body, they are one in soul through the affection of love. Love transforms the lover into the object loved. Where two friends have one soul, there can be no secret between them. My Truth said: 'I will come and we will dwell together,' and this is the truth." (CS, 146)

Jesus said to Saint Margaret of Cortona one day after she had received Holy Communion: "My child, because you have so devoutly assisted at the Divine Office in honor of all My saints, they shall each petition for you some share in their own distinguishing virtue. The Seraphim shall endow you with their ardors; the other angels will each bestow the gift proper to their own order upon you. The prophet will give you the gift of prophecy.

"In your praises keep to your custom of praising in the first place My Godhead and the mystery of My Incarnation; then render praise to My Virgin Mother and after her to your father the Blessed Francis [of Assisi].

"You have served Me according to external precepts, and as much by fear as by love, but the times draw near when you shall serve Me with all your body and soul according to the interior light I shall give you. Then My angel will instruct you both concerning those persons with whom you must not converse and concerning those whom you should honor or instruct. At no time have you been as jealous for My honor as I, your Spouse, am for your salvation." (MC, 121–122)

God the Father said to Catherine: "Love of Me and of [your] neighbor are one and the same thing." (CS, 45)

Jesus told Saint Bridget of Sweden He had been wounded, to which Bridget responded: "O Lord, who has done this to You?"

Jesus replied, "Those who scorn Me and neglect My love; they have done this to Me." (BS, 73)

Jesus said to Bridget: "I myself entered a virginal womb so that I, the invisible God, might be made visible and lost humanity might be liberated. I could quite well, indeed, have taken on another form, but it would not have been justice in God if form were not given for form and nature for nature, and if the manner of satisfaction did not accord with the manner of fault. Moreover, which of the wise could have believed or guessed that I, God almighty, would will so to humble Myself that I would take on the sackcloth of humanity, except for the fact of My incomprehensible love, because of which I willed to live visibly with man? I, God—who am love itself and who hate none of the things that I have made—arranged to give man not only My best gifts, but also Myself, as his price and his prize, so that all the proud and all the devils might be cast into confusion." (BS, 121–122)

Since the Lord had promised to answer all her prayers, Margaret began to pray for the people of Cortona. To prove the fidelity of His promise, the Lord replied. "My child, though on account of their deeds the people of Cortona deserve the evils which threaten them, nevertheless, because of their love of you and the reverence in which they hold you, I shall especially incline to them, and they shall not suffer the evils they fear. A similar grace I shall grant to all who love and protect you for My sake." (MC, 150)

Catherine received the stigmata while in Pisa, Italy. After receiving Holy Communion one day, she was overtaken by ecstasy at having been privileged to receive Our Lord. Her face began to shine before those present, and after recovering her senses, called for Blessed Raymond of Capua, her confessor. When he arrived, she related to him the following:

"You must know, Father, that by the mercy of the Lord Jesus I now bear in my body His stigmata. I saw the Lord fixed to the cross coming toward me in a great light, and such was the impulse of my soul to go and meet its Creator that it forced the body to rise up. Then from the scars of His most sacred wounds, I saw five rays of blood coming down toward me, to my hands, my feet and my heart. Realizing what was to happen, I exclaimed, "O Lord God, I beg You, do not let the scars show on the outside of my body!" As I said this, before the rays reached me, their color changed from blood red to the color of light, and in the form of pure light they arrived at the five points of my body: hands, feet and heart."

Blessed Raymond asked her if she felt any pain, and she replied: "I feel such pain at those five points especially in my heart, that if the Lord does not perform another miracle, I do not see how I can possibly go on, and within a few days I shall be dead." *Blessed Raymond, along with the others present, prayed to the Lord that He would take away the pain from the stigmata, and the Lord immediately complied, removing all pain and displeasure from the wounds. Saint Catherine, along with Saint Mary Magdalene de Pazzi and Saint Mary Frances of the Five Wounds of Jesus, is one of only a few known saints who has received the invisible stigmata.* (CS, p. ?)

Love of Neighbor

God the Father said to Saint Catherine of Siena: "I could easily have created men possessed of all that they should need both for body and soul, but I wish that one should have need of the other, and that they should be My ministers to administer the graces and the gifts that they have received from Me. Whether man wants to or not, he cannot help making an act of love. It is true, however, that that act, unless made through love of Me, profits him nothing so far as grace is concerned. See then, that I have made men My ministers, and placed them in diverse stations and various ranks, in order that they may make use of the virtue of love." (CS, 47)

God the Father said to Catherine: "I show you that in My house are many mansions, and I wish for nothing other than love, for in the love of Me is fulfilled and completed the love of the neighbor and the law is observed." (CS, 47)

God the Father said to Catherine: "The soul that knows Me immediately expands to the love of her neighbor, because she sees that I love that neighbor totally. So she loves the object [of My love] still more which she sees Me loving. . . . For as I have said to you, you can perform all virtues by means of your neighbor." (CS, 194)

God the Father said to Catherine: "I loved you without being loved by you before you existed. It was indeed love that moved Me to create you in My own image and likeness. This love you cannot repay to Me. But you can pay it to My rational creature, loving your neighbor without being loved by him, and without consideration of your own advantage . . . loving him solely for the praise and glory of My name, since he has been loved by Me. In this manner you will fulfill the commandment of the law: to love Me above everything, and your neighbor as yourselves." (CS, 194–195)

Jesus said to Saint Bridget of Sweden: "If someone knows how to cure and practices medicine for the sake of worldly repayment, he will receive no recompense from Me. But if someone practices medicine for love of Me and for My honor, then I am obligated to give him recompense. . . . If, however, led by natural love, [a physician] coddles [the sick] and raises them up in the world for his own comfort and for worldly honor, he is not to hope for recompense from Me. But if, like a good physician, he thinks of them wisely and says to himself: 'These people are sick and need medicine.' Therefore, although to them My remedy may seem bitter, nevertheless—because it is healthful—I will give it to them in order that they may not die a hard death. Therefore, while restraining them, I shall give them food lest they faint from hunger; and I shall give them clothes that they may walk honestly in accord with their station; I shall keep them under My regimen that they may not become insolent; I shall also provide for their other needs in order that they may not be lifted up by pride or grow dissolute through presumption or have occasion to do harm to others. Such a physician as this will have a large recompense from Me, for such admonishment is pleasing to Me . . ." (BS, 114–116)

Mary

Jesus said to Saint Bridget of Sweden regarding the Virgin Mary: "From eternity, it was predetermined in the Godhead that as no one was found comparable to her in charity, so too no one would be her equal in grace and blessing." (BS, 116)

Jesus said to Mary while also speaking to Bridget: "To me, this place of your womb—the spiritual as well as the corporeal—was so desirable and your soul was so pleasing that I did not disdain to come down to you from high Heaven and tarry within you. No! This deed was My sweetest delight." (BS, 120)

Jesus said to Bridget: "This Virgin so loved and desired Me that there was no hour in which she did not seek Me out of longing to become My handmaid. Therefore, she received the choice wine." (BS, 121)

Jesus said to Bridget: "Even if [Mary's] chastity had been shown by a more evident miracle, the distrustful, in their malice, would still not have ceased from the blasphemy. They distrust that a virgin conceived through the power of the Godhead because they do not attend to the fact that it is easier for Me, God, to do this than it is for the sun to penetrate glass. It is an act of My divine justice that the mystery of God's incarnation was hidden from the Devil and from mankind, to be revealed in a time of grace." (BS, 129)

God the Father said to Bridget: "Mary was a vessel clean and not clean: truly clean because she was all beautiful and because there was not found in her even enough uncleanness in which to fix the point of a needle; not clean because she came forth from Adam's root and was born of sinners although herself conceived without sin in order that, of her, My Son might be born without sin." (BS, 155) *[Editor's note: This revelation was given nearly 500 years before the dogma of the Immaculate Conception was declared.]*

In Naples, the Virgin Mary appeared to Bridget and said: "I, who speak to you, am the Queen of Heaven. I am, as it were, a gardener of this world, for when a gardener sees the rise of a strong wind harmful to the little plants and trees of his garden, at once he runs to them quickly and binds them fast with sturdy stakes as well as he can. And thus he comes to their aid, in various ways according to his ability, lest they be broken by the rushing wind or wretchedly uprooted. I, the Mother of mercy, do the same in the garden of the world." (BS, 212)

A beautiful voice said to Bridget: "I am the one who bore God's Son, the true God Jesus Christ." (BS, 11)

The Virgin Mary appeared to Bridget and said: "Because of the exceeding love that you have for me, I tell you that [as a reward] you will go to Jerusalem when it pleases my Son, and then you will go also to Bethlehem, and then I will show you how I gave birth to my Son, Jesus Christ." (BS, 93)

God the Father spoke to Bridget about the Virgin Mary's role as a perfect vessel to carry His Son Jesus: "That vessel of which I spoke to you was Mary, Joachim's daughter, the mother of Christ's human nature. She was indeed a vessel closed and not closed: Just as a torrent—wishing to enter a vessel opposed to it and not being able—seeks other ways in and out, so the Devil, like a torrent of vices, wished to approach Mary's heart by means of all his inventions. But he never was able to incline her soul toward even the slightest sin because it had been closed against his temptations, for the torrent of My Spirit had flowed into her heart and filled her with special grace." (BS, 155–156)

During Jesus's lengthy, intimate conversations with Saint Margaret of Cortona, He was also slowly but deliberately leading her soul into the realm of Heaven before the throne of the Mother of God. When Margaret asked Him why He was doing this, Jesus said to her: "I have done this so that you could more familiarly commend yourself to My Mother, the Queen of Heaven, and to the saints who assist at the throne of their King."

Margaret then turned to the Mother of Our Lord and said: "O Lady of the Heavens, and Advocate of the world! O Mother of my God! Your Son, my leader, has led me to you."

Our Lady answered Margaret: "And I receive you and your prayers. You are a daughter whom I commend to the Creator, my Son, with continuous intercession."

Upon hearing Mary say this, Margaret was elated, and continued: "My Lady, I sometimes wonder why it is that I am never blessed to converse with you. Is it because in my fervent search for your Son I do not hear your voice?"

Mary answered her: "Daughter, whoever seeks my only Son and Lord, seeks me; whoever has Him, has me." *Margaret then thanked Our Lady for her protection.*

After Margaret returned from her state of ecstasy and was back in her own home, an angel came and stood by her, comforting her. She and the angel conversed for some time, discussing the virtues of the elect. (MC, 207–208)

Mercy

While in prayer one day, Saint Catherine of Siena said to the Lord: "Your mercy compels You to give even more to mankind, namely, to leave Yourself to him in food. This is so that we weak ones should have comfort, and the ignorant who commemorate You should not lose the memory of Your gifts. Every day You give Yourself to mankind, representing Yourself in the Sacrament of the Altar, in the body of your holy Church. What has done this? Your Mercy. Oh Divine Mercy! My heart suffocates in thinking of You. Every way

I turn my thoughts, I find nothing but Mercy. Oh, Eternal Father! Forgive my ignorance that I presume to chatter to You. But the love of Your Mercy will be my excuse before the face of Your loving kindness." *The Lord said in response:* "My mercy is without any comparison, far more than you can see because your sight is imperfect, but My mercy [is] perfect and infinite." (CS, 91–92)

God the Father spoke about the state of souls that have died in despair, saying that the gravest error a soul can make is to believe that its sins are greater than the mercy of God. The Eternal Father spoke about the great and unpardonable sin of despair: "This is that sin which is neither pardoned here [on earth] nor there [in the afterlife]. The soul does not depreciate My mercy by being pardoned. This sin [of despair] is graver to Me than all the other sins that the soul has committed. The despair of Judas displeased Me more and was more grave to My Son than was his betrayal of Him. [These souls] are reproved of this false idea, which is to have believed their sin to be greater than My mercy." (CS, 103–104)

God the Father said to Catherine: "The righteous, who have lived in charity and died in love, if they have lived perfectly in virtue, illuminated with the light of faith, with perfect hope in the Blood of the Lamb, when the extremity of death comes will see the good which I have prepared for them. They will embrace it with the arms of love, holding fast with pressure of love to Me, the supreme and eternal good. They will taste eternal life before they have left the mortal body, that is, before the soul be separated from the body. Others who have passed their lives and have arrived at the last extremity of death with *ordinary charity*—(not in great perfection)—will embrace My mercy with the same light of faith and hope that had those perfect ones. However, in them it is imperfect. Since they were imperfect, they forced My mercy, counting My mercy greater than their sins. The wicked sinners do just the opposite. Seeing with desperation their destination, they embrace it with hatred. . . ." (CS, 120–121)

God the Father spoke to Catherine about souls that lose hope in God's mercy: "This final sin of despair is much more displeasing to Me, and injures them much more than all the other sins which they have committed. . . . As I have said to you, My mercy is greater by comparison than all the sins which any creature can commit. It greatly displeased Me that they should consider their sins to be greater." (CS, 267–268)

Catherine once prayed that God would remove darkness and persecutions from the Church by afflicting her instead. The Lord responded, saying that satisfaction for sin comes not solely by this means, but through afflictions united with the desires of the soul and the contrition of the heart. The Lord also said: "Another request you made to Me was that I should show mercy to the world. I have told you that I wish to show mercy to the world, proving to you that mercy is My special attribute. Through the mercy and the inestimable love which I have for mankind, I sent to the earth the Word, My only-begotten Son." (CS, 326–327)

Jesus said to Saint Bridget of Sweden: "If My friends want to be reconciled with My grace and friendship, they must make penance and have contrition [with] all their heart for having offended Me, their Creator and [Redeemer]." (BS, 41)

Jesus said to Bridget: "Why are you disturbed because I put up with that man so patiently? Do you not know that it is a grave thing to burn eternally? Therefore, even to the last point I [put up with] him, in order that in him My justice may be manifested to others." (BS, 153–154)

Regarding souls who seek and desire conversion, the Virgin Mary said to Bridget: "Know that, even so, all those who want to amend their lives will obtain mercy from God." (BS, 171)

Jesus said to Bridget: "Know for a certainty that if any one of you wills to correct himself, amend his life, and humbly turn back to Me, then like a loving shepherd I shall joyfully run out to meet him, lifting him onto My shoulders and personally carrying him back to My sheep. For by My shoulders I mean that if anyone amends his life, he will share in the benefit of My passion and death, which I endured in My body and shoulders, and he will receive with Me eternal consolation in the kingdom of Heaven." (BS, 198)

Jesus said to Bridget: "My mercy is this: namely, that none of My very enemies is so thorough or so great a sinner that My mercy would be denied him if he were to ask for it humbly and wholeheartedly. Therefore, My enemies must do three things if they wish to reconcile themselves to My grace and friendship. The first is that with all their heart they repent and have contrition because they have offended Me, their Creator and Redeemer. The second thing is confession—clean, frequent, and humble—which they must make before their confessor. . . . The third thing is that after they have thus performed these things with devotion and perfect charity, they are to go to communion and receive and consume My Body with the intention of never falling back into former sins but of persevering in good even to the end. If anyone, therefore, amends his life in this manner, at once I will run out to meet him as a loving father runs to meet his wayward son, and I will receive him into My grace more gladly than he himself could have asked or thought. And then I will be in him, and he in Me, and he shall live with Me and rejoice forever." (BS, 210–211)

Mortal Sin

God the Father said to Saint Catherine of Siena: "Open the eye of your intellect and wonder at those who voluntarily drown themselves and at the baseness to which they have fallen by their fault. At first they became weak. This was when they conceived mortal sin in their minds. They then bring it forth and [as a result] lose the life of grace. Just as a corpse can have no feeling or movement of itself—only when it is moved and lifted by others—in just the same way those who are drowned in the stream of an unbridled love of the world are dead to grace." (CS, 92–93)

God the Father said to Catherine: "See that some of the fruits [of mortal sinners] are the food of beasts who live impurely, using their body and their mind like a swine who wallows in mud. In the very same way they wallow in the mire of sensuality. Oh, ugly soul, where have you left your dignity? You were made [as a] sister to the angels, and now you have become a brute beast." (CS, 94)

God the Father said to Catherine: "Oh, how many are the sins that come of the accursed sin of avarice. How many homicides and thefts, and how much pillage with unlawful gain, and cruelty of heart and injustice! It kills the soul and makes her the slave of riches, so that she cares not to observe My commandments." (CS, 95–96)

God the Father said to Catherine: "Oh, miserable vices that destroy the Heaven of the soul. Heaven I call her (the soul) because I made her to be so, living in her at first by grace and hiding Myself within her, and making of her a mansion through love. Now she has separated herself from Me, like an adulteress, loving herself and creatures more than Me. She has made a god of herself, persecuting Me with many different sins. She does this because she does not consider the benefit of the Blood that was shed with so great a fire of love." (CS, 97)

God the Father said to Catherine: "Because their heart is rotten, wicked men, standing in self-love, impurity, pride, avarice, and founded in envy . . . are forever scandalized at Me and My servants, whom they judge to be practicing virtues with hypocrisy. With their discernment spoiled, good things seem evil to them, and bad things—that is to say, disorderly living—seems good to them. Oh how blind is the human generation that will not consider its own dignity! From being great you have become small; from a ruler you have become a slave and [indentured] in the vilest service that can be had. This is because you are the servant and slave of sin, and have become like what you serve. Sin is nothing [to you]. You, then, have become nothing; it has deprived you of life, and it has given you death." (CS, 99)

Obedience

God the Father said to Saint Catherine of Siena: "Obedience is of such excellence that you all derive grace from it, just as from disobedience you all derive death. . . . I have already told you that this word is the key which opens Heaven, the key which My Son placed in the hands of His vicar. This vicar placed it in the hands of everyone who receives holy Baptism, promising therein to renounce the world and all its pomps and delights, and to obey. If a man does not unlock the gate of Heaven by means of this key, in the light of faith and with the hand of love, he will never enter there, in spite of its having been opened by the Word [Jesus]." (CS, 286)

A converted soul who practices obedience, God the Father said to Catherine, does not suffer or feel hatred toward those who injure them. This person "feels no hatred when injured, because he wishes to obey the precept of forgiveness. Obedience has ordered him to desire Me alone, who can and will satisfy all his desires if he strips himself of worldly riches. And so in all things which would be too long to relate, he who has chosen as spouse queen obedience, the appointed key of Heaven, finds peace and quiet." (CS, 288–289)

Regarding the virtue of obedience, God the Father said to Catherine: "My Providence, the Word, repaired the key of obedience. But worldly men, devoid of every virtue, do just the opposite. They, like unbridled horses without the bit of obedience, go from bad to worse, from sin to sin, from misery to misery, from darkness to darkness, from death to death, until they finally reach the edge of the ditch of death, gnawed by the worm of their conscience Though it is true that they can obey the precepts of the law . . . it is very hard for them to do so because of their long habit of sin. So let no man trust in this, putting off his finding of the key of obedience to the moment of his death. For although everyone may and should hope [in eternal life] as long as he has life, he should not put such trust in this hope as to delay repentance." (CS, 290)

God the Father said to Catherine: "I have appointed you all to labor in the vineyard of obedience in different ways. Every man will receive a reward according to the measure of his love, and not according to the work he does or the length of time for which he works. He who comes early will not have more than he who comes late. . . . My Truth showed you in this way that you are rewarded not according to time or work, but according to the measure of your love. . . . By love of obedience, then, does the soul receive her merit, filling the vessel of her heart in Me." (CS, 320–321)

Jesus said to Saint Bridget of Sweden: "Just as it says in My gospel: 'Blessed are they who hear the words of God,' so I say now: 'Blessed are they who now hear My words and will perform them in deed.' Nevertheless, know that after your passing, more [people] will receive My words and will follow them with sweetness, for they are not like a flower that will fall but like a fruit that lasts for eternity." (BS, 95)

Jesus said to Bridget: "Hearken, all you My enemies who live in the world, for to My friends who follow My will, I am not speaking . . . I complain because you have withdrawn from Me and have put faith in the Devil, My enemy. You have abandoned My Commandments and you follow the will of the Devil and you obey his suggestions. You do not attend to the fact that I, the unchanging and eternal God, your Creator, came down from Heaven to a Virgin and took flesh from her and lived with you. Through My own self, I opened the way for you and showed the counsels by which you might go to

Heaven. I was stripped and scourged and crowned with thorns and so forcefully extended on the cross that, as it were, all the sinews and joints of My body were being undone. I heard all insults and endured a most contemptible death and most bitter heartache for the sake of your salvation. . . . Nevertheless, O My enemies, because I have redeemed you with My blood and because I am in quest of nothing but your souls, therefore return to Me even now with humility and I will gladly receive you as My children. Shake off from you the Devil's yoke and recall My charity, and you shall see in your conscience that I am sweet and meek." (BS, 216–217)

One Sunday, when Saint Margaret of Cortona was feeling great desolation of spirit because Jesus seemed no longer with her, she cried out to Him, "How is this, that though I feel You present in my soul, my soul does not hear not Your voice? O You, whose voice softens and refreshes my inmost being! Are You silent because of some fault of mine?"

The Lord said to her, "O disobedient one! Why did you hesitate to obey your confessor when he bade you to go receive Communion?"

Margaret replied, "Lord! For this reason I did not obey: because I thought myself destitute of every virtue since the joy of Your presence was taken from me. Yet if in this I have offended Your kindness, I am sorry."

The Lord then said to Margaret, "Not because of your reverence and fear was I offended, but because you did not obey. And I command you, My child, as often as you are told to do anything by your confessor, to obey him, because by special grace I have enlightened him in regard to guide you in the ordering of your life." (MC, 162–164)

God the Father spoke to Catherine about how certain souls wish to advance in perfection and move from general obedience to a more particular obedience. He said: "There are some, My dearest daughter, in whom the sweet and amorous fire of love toward obedience burns so high (which cannot exist without contempt for one's self, so that when the fire increases so does this self-contempt) that they are not content to observe the precepts of the law [of love] with a general obedience—as you are all obliged to do if you will have life and not death—but take upon themselves a particular obedience, following the greatest perfection, so that they become observers of the counsels both in deed and in thought. These people wish to bind themselves more tightly through self-contempt, and in order to restrain everything, [they restrain] their own will. They either place themselves under the yoke of obedience in holy religion, or, without entering religion, they bind themselves to some creature, submitting their will to his so as more expeditiously to unlock the door of Heaven. These are they, as I have told you, who have chosen the most perfect obedience." (CS, 293)

After Margaret had been led by Jesus to seek greater perfection, He spoke to her saying: "My child, it has been My pleasure that you should dwell in the house you are in, but now I wish you would no longer remain here or return to your former house with friends. Go and seek dwelling in the Rocca [the chief fortress defending Cortona]."

Knowing the friars would not approve of the change of location both because of the long distance from their house and the fear that if Margaret died there, her body would not be buried in their church, the Lord therefore said to Margaret: "Do not let the friars be concerned about your burial, but let them rest assured that no matter where you shall die, your body shall be given back to them. Tell the friars who visit you that they must take care of you because of love for Me who for man's sake came down from Heaven, not to receive honor and joy, but to be scoffed at and suffer."

On another occasion, Jesus said: "Though I gave them [the friars] to you as earthly guides, it is I who have been and still am the guide of your soul. I made Myself the leader on your journey after I saved you from the deep into which your love of the world led you. I was the beginning of your conversion and the rule by which your conversion was perfected; and I will be both the means of your Salvation and its End. It is I who have led you to this house under the Rocca, because there you will offend Me less and serve Me better." (MC, 115–117)

Saint Francis of Assisi appeared to Bridget in Rome on his feast day and said: "Come into my chamber to eat and drink with me." *She made a pilgrimage to Assisi, stayed there for five days, and then returned to Rome. Saint Francis appeared to her again and said:* "Welcome! For I invited you into my chamber to eat and drink with me. Know now that this building is not the chamber that I mentioned to you. No, my chamber is true obedience, to which I have always so held that I never endured to be without an instructor. For I continually had with me a priest whose every instruction I humbly obeyed, and this was my chamber. Therefore, do likewise, for this is pleasing to God. My food, however, whereby I was refreshed with delight, was the fact that I most willingly drew my neighbors away from the vanities of worldly life to serve God with whole of their hearts; and I then swallowed that joy as if it were the sweetest morsels. My drink, however, was that joy I had while I saw some whom I converted loving God, devoting themselves with all their strength to prayer and contemplation, teaching others to live good lives, and imitating true poverty. Behold daughter: that drink so gladdened my soul that, for me, all things in the world lost their taste. Enter, therefore, into this chamber of mine; and eat this, my food; and drink this drink with me. Drink it so that you may be refreshed with God eternally." (BS, 161)

The Passion of Christ

Saint Margaret of Cortona sought the Lord in prayer, asking that He grant her to be able to feel some of the sorrow which pierced the heart of His mother standing beside the cross. Christ said to her, "At sunrise you shall go as usual to the church of My friars, and there the scenes of My passion will be brought before you, and you shall experience at the sight of it such anguish and bitterness and pain as you have never yet known or felt."

That day, while at the Franciscan church, Margaret saw scenes from the Passion of Jesus, exclaiming as she did: "Now He is brought forth from the palace!" "Now He is being taken out of the gate!" "Now Simon is forced to help Him!" "Now they are putting the thieves one on each side of my Lord!"

She continued with her exclamations until the visions ended, and then coming to herself, realized that the townspeople had entered the church and were observing her. She was struck with remorse, out of fear they would think she was creating a spectacle for reasons of vanity. But Jesus calmed her fears, saying, "Be not afraid, and have no scruple concerning what has been done in you this day, for I have made you to be a mirror for sinners, even the most obstinate, that through you they may learn how freely My mercy is opened out to them that they may be saved." (MC, 176–181)

Jesus told Saint Bridget of Sweden to give the following instruction to Queen Joanna of Naples: "Every day, at fixed times, she should remember God's wounds and His passion, for by this means the love of God is renewed in the heart." (BS, 174)

Peace

One day Saint Margaret of Cortona was in prayer, attempting to assist her confessor who was trying to quell turbulence in the streets of Cortona. She received from Jesus this response to her prayers: "My child, tell your confessor that he should first strive to establish peace among the inhabitants of [Cortona]. Then, afterwards, let him work for peace between Cortona and the neighboring cities. And tell him that the time will come when the citizens will remember his words and receive them more readily than [they do] now."

While her confessor was also laboring to put an end to a private feud, the Devil appeared to Margaret and told her that he would fight against her confessor's attempts. He then dealt the confessor such a setback that without the timely intervention of Jesus, the confessor would have been too afraid to continue.

Jesus gave the confessor His blessing after Margaret's outpouring of prayers on the friar's behalf. Jesus also encouraged the confessor not to fear, because He was with him. So the confessor was greatly encouraged to persevere in his labors for peace.

Undeterred, the Devil still tried to sow discord. He managed to set the confessor against Margaret, but she carried on and continued her prayers for the friar. Jesus then spoke to Margaret regarding this situation, telling her: "Inform your confessor I wish his life to be that of an apostle; let him find comfort in Me and bring Me all his troubles. When he sets himself to guide souls, let him not be too anxious. Also, he should not pay any attention when people murmur against him. For many also murmured bitterly against Me, their creator. And tell him to consider diligently how many came to crucify Me in the hour of My passion who afterwards came to adore Me. Tell him not to slacken in his labors, but continue on to the end, seeking to establish peace in the city, for I am with him."

On another day Jesus said to Margaret: "My child, what would you say if the time came when the citizens of Cortona would bless the alms they give you, seeing that you are a voice in the wilderness to call them to peace? For I will that you cry out to Cortona, 'Peace among men.' And truly you are sent as a messenger of peace. I grant this grace to the citizens of Cortona because of the reverent devotion they've shown to you. So tell your confessor to preach publicly in Cortona the message of peace. Also, in My name, [ask him] to invite the people to mutual trust and concord."

Margaret worried about delusions of the Devil, since he had the ability to feign virtue. But the Lord assured her and asked of her: "My child, [My] voice in the wilderness, do as I bid you and tell your confessor that he can confidently invite the people to make peace. Let him remind them how I, the creator of all things that are, the Lord Almighty, made peace with My persecutors. [Have him] tell them how I made peace with those who delivered Me up to my enemies and [with] those who derided Me and tore off My garments and scourged Me; how I made peace with those who spat in My face and struck Me; with those who blindfolded Me and crowned Me with thorns; who crucified Me and gave Me vinegar to drink, and who pierced My side; yes, even with those who denied Me.

[Remind them] how I made peace when, because of the bitterness of My sufferings, My human nature, so sensitively formed, was [close to the breaking point]. I therefore command the people of Cortona to put aside all feuds whatsoever and immediately make peace, so that they will not, in condemning My words, fall under the judgment of My wrath."

Margaret protested her unworthiness as an intermediary, but the Lord responded: "I tell you, announce the words of peace, calling upon Cortona to lay aside its quarrels. In no way will their defects hinder their peace. For I, your Redeemer, have put you in the wilderness of this world as a voice crying aloud. Your early life did indeed cry out against Me. But now, brought into the way of penance, your life cries aloud that I am full of mercy, and sinners hear and learn from you." (MC, 266–270)

Penance

God the Father said to Saint Catherine of Siena: "Works of penance performed alone without . . . virtues would please Me little. Often, indeed, if the soul does not perform penance with discretion, that is to say, if her affection be placed principally in the penance she has undertaken, her perfection will be impeded. She should rather place reliance on the affection of love, with a holy hatred of herself, accompanied by true humility and perfect patience. [These should be done] together with the other intrinsic virtues of the soul, with a hunger and desire for My honor and the salvation of souls." (CS, 50)

God the Father said to Catherine: "Penance should be [simply a] means of increasing virtue according to the needs of the individual and according to what the soul sees she can do in the measure of her own possibility. Otherwise, if the soul places her foundation on penance [alone] she will contaminate her own perfection." (CS, 51)

God the Father said to Catherine: "He who desires for My sake to mortify his body with many penances and not his own will does not give me much pleasure." (CS, 55)

One year on the eve of the feast day of Saint Mary Magdalene, Saint Margaret of Cortona had been too weak to get out of bed. Suddenly, she was filled with such fervor of spirit that those around her were amazed. She passed the evening in great joyfulness singing the praises of God, when suddenly her soul went into rapture and she beheld Saint Mary Magdalene. Mary was clothed in a silver robe and wore a crown of precious gems. She was surrounded by holy angels. While Margaret was in this ecstasy, Christ spoke to her: "My Eternal Father said of Me to John the Baptist: 'This is My beloved Son.' So I say to you of Magdalene: 'This is My beloved daughter.' And since you are in wonderment at [Magdalene's] shining raiment, know that she gained this in her solitude. *[According to tradition, after Our Lord's Resurrection, Mary Magdalene led the life of a contemplative in solitude, prayer and penance.]* And her crown of precious gems is hers because of the temptations she overcame during the time of her penance." (MC, 217–218)

Poverty

Mary said to Saint Bridget of Sweden: "Which of the saints had the sweetness of the Spirit without first experiencing bitterness? Therefore, one who craves sweetness must not flee away from things that are bitter." (BS, 107)

Regarding a certain Franciscan, Mary said to Bridget: "He is not to have an overabundance of clothing but only necessary things, according to the Rule of Saint Francis, so that pride and cupidity may not ensue; for the less costly and valuable his clothes have been, the more lavish shall be his reward." (BS, 169)

Jesus told Queen Joanna of Naples through Bridget: "She should be content with the colors and beauty by which God has adorned her face, for extraneous color is very displeasing to God." (BS, 175)

One day Jesus gave Bridget a message she was to pass on to a bishop: "Of your clothing, I advise you never to have in your possession more than three pairs at one time; everything beyond this, you should immediately give to God himself [e.g. to the Church to distribute to those in need of such things]. Of bedcovers, towels and tablecloths, keep for yourself only what is necessary and useful to you, and give the rest to God. Of silver vessels, reserve for yourself just enough for your own person and for the guests who eat at your own table. Donate the superfluous pieces to God with a cheerful mind, for the rest of your household and the guests who sit at other tables certainly can, without any embarrassment, eat and drink using vessels of tin, clay, wood or glass. For that custom which now prevails in the houses of bishops and lords of having an overly excessive abundance of gold and silver is quite harmful to souls and very repulsive to God himself, who, for our sake, subjected himself to all poverty." (BS, 179–180)

Mary said to Bridget, "But of our riches, Joseph and I reserved nothing for ourselves except for the necessities of life, for the honor of God. The rest we let go, for the love of God." (BS, 206)

Prayer

God the Father said to Saint Catherine of Siena: "For no other reason ought the soul leave off prayer [other than for obedience or for charity's sake]. During the time ordained for prayer, the Devil likes to arrive in the soul, causing much more conflict and trouble than when the soul is not occupied in prayer. This he does in order that holy prayer may become tedious to the soul." (CS, 158–159)

God the Father said to Catherine: "Know, dearest daughter, how by humble, continual and faithful prayer the soul acquires with time and perseverance every virtue. So she should persevere and never abandon prayer, either through the illusion of the Devil or her own fragility. . . . The Devil often places himself upon the tongues of creatures, causing them to chatter nonsensically, with the purpose of preventing the prayer of the soul." (CS, 159)

God the Father said to Catherine: "Perfect prayer is not attained through many words, but through affection of desire. The soul raises herself up to Me with knowledge of herself and of My mercy, seasoning one with the other. Thus she will exercise together mental and vocal prayer. Just as the active and the contemplative life are one, so are they." (CS, 166)

God the Father said to Catherine: "Each one, according to his condition, ought to exert himself for the salvation of souls, for this exercise lies at the root of a holy will. Whatever may contribute by words or deeds toward the salvation of your neighbor is virtually a prayer." (CS, 166)

Regarding true poverty and obedience, virtues practiced in ages past by religious orders, God the Father said: "See how in the days when the religious orders lived virtuously, blossoming with true poverty and fraternal charity, their temporal substance never failed them, but they had more than their needs demanded. But because the stench of self-love has entered and caused each to keep his private possessions and to fail in obedience, their temporal substance has failed, and the more they possess, to the greater destitution do they come." (CS, 296)

Jesus told Saint Bridget of Sweden why some prayers are not answered: "I am like a mother who sees her son making a request contrary to his welfare and puts off listening to his petition while stemming his tears with some indignation. Indeed, such indignation is not anger but great mercy. Thus, I, God, do not always hear [i.e. answer] My friends because I see—better than they themselves would see—the things that are more useful for their welfare. Did not Paul and others pray with energy and yet were not heard? . . . Just as the Devil does not blush to tempt his own because he sees that they are quite prompt in sinning, so for a time I do not spare My elect because I see that they are prepared for all good." (BS, 145)

Priests

Jesus said through Saint Bridget of Sweden to a bishop: "I advise you that, if you would have God's friendship, neither you, nor any other bishop acting on your behalf, should be willing to promote anyone to sacred orders unless he has first been diligently examined by good clerics and has been found to be so suitable in his life and character that, by the testimony of wise and truthful men, he is declared worthy to receive such an office." (BS, 178)

Jesus spoke to Bridget regarding His Passion, complaining that "the world's princes are not attentive, nor do they consider the places in which I was born and I suffered." *He said this was the case even among the prelates of the Church.* "They gaze at earthly delights with greater eagerness and pleasure than at My death and My Passion and My wounds. Therefore, I shall now send My words through you, and if they do not change their hearts and turn them toward Me, they will be condemned along with those who divided My clothing and over My garment cast lots." (BS, 191)

Jesus instructed Bridget to write the following to the king of Cyprus and his uncle, the prince of Antioch: "You should tell all the prelates that they must effectively and frequently admonish all their clerics, namely the rectors of churches, that each of them is to inquire diligently in his parish as to whether there be any of his parishioners who persist in living wickedly in public sins, causing offense to God and contempt for Holy Mother Church. Any such people whom they find living impudently in their public sins they are to forewarn with effective admonishments concerning the peril of their souls, and they are to teach them such measures and spiritual remedies by means of which they can and must humbly amend their lives." (BS, 196)

God the Father said to Saint Catherine of Siena: "I will speak to you, dearest daughter, of the dignity of priests. I have placed them where they are through My goodness, over and above the general love which I have had to My creatures. I have created you in My image and likeness, and re-created you all to the life of grace in the Blood of My only-begotten Son. From this you have arrived at such excellence, through the union which I made of My Deity with human nature. In this you have greater dignity and excellence than the angels. . . . I took on your human nature [through Jesus] and not that of the angels. So as I have said to you, I, God, have become man, and man has become God by the union of My Divine nature with your human nature. This greatness is given in general to all rational creatures. But among these I have especially chosen My ministers for the sake of your salvation, so that through them the Blood of the humble and immaculate Lamb, My only-begotten Son, may be administered to you." (CS, 228)

God the Father said to Catherine: "I have told you all this, dearest daughter, so that you can better recognize the dignity to which I have called My priests; this, so that your grief at their failures and shortcomings might be more intense. If they themselves considered their own dignity, they would not be in the darkness of mortal sin, or defile the face of their soul. They would not only realize their offenses against Me, but even if they gave their bodies to be burned they would not repay the tremendous grace and favor which they have received. No greater dignity exists in this life. They are My anointed ones, and I call them My Christs." (CS, 239–240)

Regarding priests who have fallen from grace and are living in sin, God the Father said to Catherine: "You should love [priests] by reason of the virtue and dignity of the Sacrament. By reason of that very virtue and dignity you should hate the defects of those who live miserably in sin. But do not appoint yourselves their judges, which I forbid, because they are My Christs, and you ought to love and reverence the authority which I have given them. You well know that if a filthy and badly dressed person brought you a great treasure from which you obtained life, you would not hate the bearer, however ragged and filthy he might be.

"It is not My will that they should be in this state. You should pray for them and not judge them, leaving their judgment to Me. Moved by your prayers, I will do them mercy if they will only receive it. But if they do not correct their life, their dignity will be the cause of their ruin. If they do not accept the breadth of My mercy, I, the Supreme Judge, shall terribly condemn them at their last extremity and they will be sent to the eternal fire." (CS, 256, 258)

God the Father said to Catherine: "Oh! How happy are the souls [of priests] when they come to the extremity of death! For they have been the defenders and preachers of the faith to their neighbor. They have incarnated this faith in their very marrow, and with it they see their place of repose in Me. The hope with which they have lived, confiding in My providence [and living] in voluntary poverty, causes them now to lift their confidence towards Me with great delight. . . . So, they gloriously pass, bathed in the Blood, with hunger for the salvation of souls, all on fire with love for their neighbor. They pass through the door of the Word and enter into Me. By My goodness each one is arranged in his place, and to each one is measured according to the love he has measured to Me." (CS, 262–264)

The Virgin Mary appeared to Bridget and said: "Say to that same bishop that because he is accustomed to begin all his sermons with praise of Me and because his judgment of another person was made with charity rather than envy, his charity thus merits consolation. Tell him, therefore, that I want to be a mother to him and that I want to present his soul to God." (BS, 89)

Once, the Virgin Mary was speaking to Bridget regarding Lord Elzear, a man who was considering becoming a cleric. Mary gave counsel regarding what he should say and do in order to become holy. "Say that you [Bridget] would be willing to endure all the tribulation of the flesh rather than lose your chastity. Answer also that you want to acquire knowledge and the arts for the honor of God and the defense of the Catholic faith, for the strengthening of good people and for the correction of the erring and of all who need your advice and teaching; and say that you do not wish to desire anything in this life beyond sustenance for your body and for the household truly necessary to you and not overly enlarged for the sake of vainglory. Say also that, if perchance Divine Providence were to confer on you some added dignity, you desire to order all things wisely for the benefit of your neighbor and for the honor of God." (BS, 165–166)

The Virgin Mary said: "Tell him [a friar] also, on My behalf, what he will answer to those who say that the Pope is not the true Pope and that it is not the true Body of Jesus Christ My Son that the priests confect on the altar. He should answer those heretics in this way: 'You have turned the backs of your heads to God, and thus you do not see Him. Turn therefore to Him your faces, and then you will be able to see Him. [A] Pope who is without heresy—no matter how stained he be with other sins—is never so wicked as a result of these sins and his other bad deeds that there would not always be in him full authority through blessed Peter. . . . For a similar reason, I also say that all those priests who are not heretical—although otherwise full of many other sins—are true priests and truly confect the Body of Christ My Son. Truly they touch God in their hands on the altar and administer the other Sacraments even though, because of their sins and evil deeds, they are unworthy of Heavenly glory in God's sight." (BS, 170)

The Virgin Mary gave this message to Bridget to be relayed to a Franciscan friar, "Say to my friend the friar that it is not licit [i.e. appropriate] for you to know whether the soul of Pope John XXII is in Hell or in Heaven. Nor indeed is it licit for you to know anything about the sins that the same Pope took with him when, after his death, he came before God's judgment. But tell the same friar that those decretals that the same Pope John made or established concerning Christ's private property contain no error in the Catholic faith nor any heresy." (BS, 170)

The Virgin Mary said to Bridget: "Through God's preordinance and his judgment, it has been justly ordained that priests who do not live in chastity and continence of the flesh are cursed and excommunicated before God and deserve to be deprived of their priestly office. But still, if they truthfully amend their lives with the true purpose of not sinning further, they will obtain mercy from God." (BS, 172–173)

Jesus said to Bridget: "Tell him [the Neapolitan archbishop] that if he wishes to be called a bishop in the justice of the divine judgment, he must not imitate the manners and customs of many who are now rulers of the Church. I took on a human body from a virgin in order that by words and deeds I might fulfill the law which, from eternity, had been ordained in the Godhead. I opened the gate of Heaven with My heart's blood, and I so illumined the way by My words and deeds that all might use My example in order to merit eternal life. But truly, the words that I said and the deeds that I did in the world are now almost completely forgotten and neglected. For this, no one is as much a cause as the prelates of the churches. They are full of pride, greed, and the rottenness of bodily pleasure. All of these things are contrary to My Commandments and to Holy Church's honorable statutes, which My friends established out of great devotion after My Ascension and after I had accomplished My will in the world. For those wicked prelates of the churches, who are filled with the malignity of an evil spirit, have left to mankind examples that are exceedingly harmful to souls, and therefore it is necessary for Me to exact full justice from them by doing judgment on them, abolishing them from the book of life in Heaven, and placing them beside My enemy Lucifer in Hell, in Hellish sees that shall be the seat of their perpetual excruciation. Nevertheless, you ought to know that if anyone is willing to amend himself before death by loving Me with all his heart and if he abstains from sins, then I will be prompt in showing My mercy." (BS, ?)

Jesus gave Bridget the following message to pass on to an archbishop: Constantly try as much as possible, with words and deeds, by enticing or rebuking or threatening, to work together with them [the priests] so that they may endeavor to lead a chaste life, especially since they must touch so very holy a Sacrament and, with their hands, administer it to other faithful Christians." (BS, 177–178)

Purgatory

A deceased woman appeared to Saint Bridget of Sweden who was at prayer and said, "To you shall be given understanding of spiritual things; in all things, therefore, humble yourself. And that you may know this with greater certainty, behold, I give to you a threefold sign. The first is that I have been gravely purged for the stubbornness of my conscience. The second: that my husband, who is not my husband, now seeks something carnal—namely, carnal intercourse with another woman in opposition to God—and it will be for him and his posterity a cause of tribulation. The third is that you will cross the sea and you will die in a glorious place: in Rome."

Later, the deceased woman appeared to Bridget a second time and said: "I want to inform you of my situation, for thus it pleases God that as we have loved each other while both living in the flesh, so we should now love each other in spirit. I—to speak using a similitude—have been put, as it were, in thick glass and can hear, but not yet reach, the things that I wish for. Thus I can understand and desire and hope for those everlasting joys; but I have not yet attained to the full until the glass, by God's will, becomes more thin and sheer. And this has been because two things weighed me down in the world: namely, a facility of anger; and the fact that I was not content with the things that I had, but wanted always to have more. Therefore, induce those who were my friends to have chalices made for me in which the sacrifice of my Lord Jesus Christ may be offered; and second, to have remembrance of Me made during the year [at Mass] by those who are the friends of God. For by such means I shall, without a doubt, be more quickly freed from this punishment."

Finally, this same soul appeared to Bridget a third time and said: "What I have longed for, I now have. My former torments have been consigned into oblivion, and my love is now perfect. But as for you: be obedient! For you are going to come into the society of the great." (BS, 84–85)

Due to Saint Margaret of Cortona's sanctity and her unique relationship with Our Lord, He at times permitted souls of the dead to come to her and ask for her assistance. One example among many involved two brothers from Cortona, day laborers who had been dishonest in their labor and had been murdered by robbers. They informed Margaret that through the grace of God and by a last minute act of contrition, they were fortunate to escape the fires of Hell and were currently suffering in purgatory.

They asked Margaret to go to their home and find enough possessions to make restitution to those for whom they worked. While she was praying for these brothers, as well as for others who had asked for her assistance, Jesus said to her: "Tell the Friars Minor to keep in mind the souls of the dead who suffer for their sins in purgatory. There is a vast number of these souls, larger than man can imagine. These souls are helped hardly at all by those who live on earth—even by those dear to them." (MC, 260–261)

Sins

Jesus said to Saint Bridget of Sweden: "Because of this [Satan's three greatest sins—pride, desire, and lust], he fell from Heaven, filled the earth with these sins and so violated all mankind. Therefore I took on humanity and came into the world, to annihilate his pride by My humility [and] to destroy his desire by My poverty and simplicity. And I submitted to the most immense penance of the Cross in order to annihilate his abominable lust and to open Heaven [as long as man] inserts his will to work for it, according to his ability. But now men [and] knights sin in the same manner as the Devil did before them. They take pride in their well-shaped bodies which I gave them. They overflow with their abominable lust to such a degree that they would rather kill Me, were it possible for them, than abstain from their lusts or endure My frightful justice, which threatens them for their sins." (BS, 19)

The Virgin Mary said: "Therefore the guardian [i.e., reason] must resist such delight and say this: 'Just as the Devil has hatred for all the [grace for] humanity that the Holy Spirit breathes into the hearts of human beings, so I, by the working of God's help, will have hatred for all the pomp and worldly pride that the evil spirit, with his pestilent inflammation, pours into hearts.'" (BS, 166)

God the Father said to Saint Catherine of Siena: "Oh, miserable sin of cruelty which will deprive the man who practices it of all mercy unless he turns to kindness and benevolence toward his neighbor." *God the Father said later in this dialogue with Saint Catherine that the soul, no matter how sinful, can turn from sin and seek forgiveness from God and be fully pardoned.* (CS, 42)

God the Father said to Catherine: "Sometimes the sinner brings forth insults on which often follows murder, and sometimes also [follows] impurity against the person of his neighbor, by which he becomes a brute beast full of stench. In this case he does not poison one only; [anyone who] approaches him with love or in conversation is also poisoned." (CS, 42)

God the Father said to Catherine: "Sin causes a physical and mental injury. The mental injury is already done when the sinner has conceived pleasure in the idea of sin, and hatred of virtue. . . . After he has conceived [this idea], he brings forth one sin after another against his neighbor." (CS, 41)

God the Father said to Catherine: "A secret sin is when you deprive your neighbor of that which you ought to give him; an open sin is where you perform positive acts of sin." (CS, 43)

Saint Catherine of Siena was privileged to be able to sense the presence of and even smell sin. This "odor of sin," as it is called, was a dreadful stench that she confessed was so awful in some of those who visited her that she could barely endure it. On one occasion Catherine and her confessor met a woman who was privately leading an evil life. The confessor related later: "While this woman and Catherine were talking together, I was present too, and while the woman seemed decent enough in her dress and behavior, I noticed that she was never able to look the virgin [Saint Catherine] straight in the face. Wondering at this, I took the trouble to find out who the woman was [from others], and was told that she was [a decent woman]. I mentioned this to the virgin, and she told me privately, 'If you had smelled the stink that I could smell while I was talking to her, you would have been sick.'" (CS, p. ?)

God the Father said to Catherine: "If one single sin were committed to save the whole world from Hell, or to obtain one great virtue, the motive would not be [just]. It is not lawful to perform an act of great virtue and profit to others by means of the guilt of sin." (CS, 58)

God the Father said to Catherine: "[The sinner fills his] memory with the delights of sin and with the recollection of shameful pride, avarice, self-love, hatred and unkindness to his neighbors (being also a persecutor of My servants). With these miseries he has obscured his intellect by his disoriented will. Let such as these receive the eternal pains, with their horrible stench, inasmuch as they have not satisfied for their sins with contrition and displeasure of their guilt." (CS, 37)

God the Father said to Catherine: "Your sins consist of nothing else than loving that which I hate, and in hating that which I love. I love virtue and hate vice. He who loves vice and hates virtue offends Me and is deprived of My grace." (CS, 209–210)

God the Father spoke bluntly regarding the sins that people commit, stating that oftentimes people find upon reflection that the sins against themselves are minor offenses in comparison. He said to Catherine: "Abandon the injustice, murders, hatreds, rancors, detractions, murmurings, false judgments and cruelty with your neighbors. [Stop] your thefts and treacheries, and the disordinate pleasures and delights of the world. Cut off the horns of pride. By this amputation you will extinguish the hatred which is in your heart against your neighbors. Compare the injuries which you do to Me and to your neighbor with those done to you. You will see that those done to you are but trifles." (CS, 292–293)

Jesus said to Bridget: "Could anything that comes from something unclean be clean itself? Therefore, when the first man lost the beauty of innocence because of his disobedience, he was cast out of the paradise of joy and became involved in unclean things. No one was found able, of himself, to recover his innocence. Therefore, I, the merciful God, came in the flesh and instituted Baptism, by means of which a child is liberated from uncleanness and from sin." (BS, 141)

Jesus said to Bridget: "Human beings love darkness more than light." (BS, 163)

Regarding certain friars who did not adequately follow the rules of the order and live converted lives, Mary said, "For their transgressions, [a certain friar] should charitably reprove his other brothers with good words, with salutary teachings, and, when he might be able to correct them, even with just rebukes, to the end that they may keep the rule and humbly amend their lives." (BS, 169)

God the Father said to Catherine: "There are three principal vices, namely, self-love, from which proceeds the second, that is love of reputation, whence proceeds the third, that is pride, with injustice and cruelty and other filthy and evil sins that follow upon these." (CS, 105)

Jesus said to Bridget: "What are those human beings who are My enemies doing to Me now? In truth, they have contempt for My precepts; they cast Me out of their hearts like a loathsome poison. . . . Moreover, know that just as all mortal sins are very serious, so too a venial sin is made mortal if a human being delights in it with the intention of persevering . . ." (BS, 208)

Jesus spoke to Saint Margaret of Cortona one day as a close friend in whom He felt comfortable confiding His own thoughts. He said to her, "My child, why will people bind themselves in the chains of vice, not accidentally, but deliberately and knowingly? Then, after they are bound, they [suffer exceedingly] and are drawn from sin to sin; they are beaten, yet they neither feel it nor resist.

"To you, My child, I complain because of these things and because [by these actions] the people I made as My own image become like beasts. With the wages of Hell they procure for themselves glory in this world. But the glory promised to them in their Heavenly fatherland they shun as though it were eternal torment. And yet for their sake, I was bound to the pillar and scourged. But if they, of their own will, allow themselves to be bound, let them not blame My goodness.

"My child, I have reasons for these complaints. They call the bitter sweet, and the sweet bitter. Yet, to make them free and to lift the veil from their eyes, did I not make Myself a servant and let Myself be blindfolded before Pilate and the Jews? Why then have they spurned their Creator and taken to themselves new masters from those I cast out of paradise? Why have they forgotten Me, their Creator? Why are their bonds to them so sweet that they will gladly go bound into eternal misery?

"But at the moment when they hear the words, 'Depart from Me, you wicked,' they'll be terribly distraught watching the just being taken into the Kingdom while they themselves are deprived of their infinite good and are cast into the eternal flame."

When she heard this, Margaret was torn with pity for these souls and said: "Lord, do not let Your people come to such a horrible end."

Jesus answered her, "The devils by whom they let themselves be bound scourge them daily even as wheat is beaten on the threshing floor. They have become like beasts of burden to the devils and bear the burdens put upon them, and yet they will not acknowledge that they suffer. Their lords have nothing but evil with which to repay them; they give them the only wages they can give. From these masters of theirs come pestilences. I will not prevent them, but rather I'll let them work their will, until the people and their goods are consumed."

At this, Margaret was filled with pity and begged mercy from Jesus. He responded, "I call them and they will not listen. They've become deaf to My voice. Yet I tell you that however hardened in sin a man may be, if he returns to Me with no pretense and with a sincere heart, I will receive him back into the fullness of My mercy and grace. Also, I send My angels to watch over them and frequently urge them to do penance." (MC, p. ?)

Margaret wanted to know whether God's glorious angels were willing to dwell with sinners, and Jesus replied, "Because of the abomination of sin, [angels] do not continuously abide with the sinner. But they often come to him to invite him to return to virtue, and they endeavor to bring him back to My mercy. But at their coming, the apostate spirits tremble and are enraged.

"Why do My children deceive Me and refuse to walk in the way they began? Tell the friars that they must preach My word fervently, and by their preaching open the ears of the deaf, and by their example give sight to the blind.

"My child, I delight in your humility and purity and charity. For a long time there has been no one to whom such high thoughts have been revealed. Also, at this time there is no one who suffers as you do. But fear not, for you know that it is I, your God, Who watches over you."

At another time Margaret heard Jesus asking her, "My child, do you truly believe that I am the Lord your God?"

Margaret asked Jesus why He should pose such a question. He responded to her, "Because, My child, to most men I am dead, as far as they can make Me so. I live by grace in very few. They offend Me so greatly that if I forgot that I, the true God, came to suffer for them, surely I would hiss them away from My presence when they come to communicate [with Me]. For such is the horror of their sins. When they receive Me unworthily [in Holy Communion] they again crucify Me and cause Me to drink a more bitter cup than that which the Jews offered Me.

"But as I permitted the Jews to take hold of Me and drag Me through the city to Calvary, I now also suffer injury from those who receive Me without devotion and who handle Me irreverently.

"Tell your confessor that I command him never again to give the Communion of My Body to any person, whether religious or secular, unless she first stops painting or adorning her face, or at least is prepared to do so. And [they must be ready] to obey My commandments and to do My will. For the communions of worldlings and [the way they conduct] their lives are an exceeding offense to Me.

"Woe to souls who do not stop offending Me and yet presume to receive My Body. It will go hard for them at their judgment. And as to the knowledge of souls which is given to you, know that this is a high degree of perfection, as Fra Giunta [*Margaret's spiritual director*] has told you.

"Yet prepare yourself for suffering, for many people shall come to regard you with contempt. But their evil-speaking of you shall substitute for the martyrdom which many suffered for Me in ancient days.

"And again, because of your fear of offending Me, even slight hardships will appear to you as great. But do not fear, My child, My companion, My sister, if in the sight of the world My favors are less frequently granted to you. For it will happen that the world may despise you, yet you will be made more secure in My grace.

"Tell Fra Giunta to prepare himself diligently when he says Mass, and to take comfort in adversity by recalling to mind how I suffered. Let him take diligent care to conquer himself."

On a day during the octave of the Feast of the Ascension, Margaret received the following message from Jesus, "In the presence of My Eternal Father I plead for you with that compassion which I had for Mary and Martha in their trouble. In you My life is revealed afresh.

"I tell you that the people of Cortona daily offend Me by their double-dealings and deceit, as does the entire world. If I considered only [the people of Cortona], their sins would inflame My wrath [to the point that I would] punish them. But because of My love for you, I show them mercy."

At another time, during Advent and after an awesome visit from a fiery angel who had six wings, Margaret was transfigured in ecstasy in the love of God. Then, Jesus spoke to her: "You are the one who wages a great war against My enemy. I tell you, my people have turned their thoughts from Me and have forgotten Me. They care nothing for Me. Yet even though they think of Me so cheaply and they greatly offend Me, I do not accuse them before My Father as I [accuse them now] before you. I do not list their offenses to Him so that He won't punish and destroy them. Rather, I am their advocate who tries to reverse their sentence." (MC, 202–205; 238–240; 282; 286–287)

In Margaret's age, an age similar to our own of great saints and great sinners, Jesus one day said to her, "My child, I lament a great deal over the irreverence of all the priests who daily hold Me in their hands but have no love for Me, who hardly acknowledge My presence. If they gave it a thought, they would surely know that among created things, nothing is more beautiful than the priest saying Mass. Yet, so many of them are not afraid to touch Me with stained hands, and to treat Me as less than the dust in the street."

When she heard these words, Margaret was filled with fear. Thinking about her own unworthiness to receive Holy

Communion, she said to Him, "Why then, O Lord, do You so frequently invite me—even compel me—a person so unworthy, to receive Your Sacred Body?"

Jesus answered her, "My child, I, the eternal Son of God, born into the world of a Virgin, have cleansed you from your sins. And now I bless you on the part of My Father, on My own part and on that of the Holy Spirit; and in the name, too, of My most blessed Mother." (MC, 235–236)

Spiritual Life

God the Father said to Saint Catherine of Siena: "Self-love, which destroys charity and affection toward the neighbor, is the principle and foundation of every evil. All scandals, hatred, cruelty, and every sort of trouble proceed from this perverse root of self-love." (CS, 43)

God the Father said to Catherine: "You know that every evil is founded in self-love, and that self-love is a cloud that takes away the light of reason. This reason holds in itself the light of faith, and one is not lost without the other." (CS, 130)

God the Father said to Catherine: "I created the soul in My image and likeness, giving her memory, intellect, and will. The intellect is the most noble part of the soul and is moved by and nourishes affection. The hand of love—that is, the affection—fills the memory with the remembrance of Me and of the benefits received, which it does with care and gratitude. So one power spurs on another, and the soul is nourished in the life of grace." (CS, 130)

Catherine was known to fall into ecstasy and remain motionless and without any perception of activity around her, even as a child. One day when she was still a child, while helping her father, a cloth dyer, she went into ecstasy and lost all motion as well as sensory experience. She was stationed at the spit, but no longer was turning the handle. Her sister-in-law, Lisa, who was accustomed to seeing Catherine's elevated mystical experiences, took her place and proceeded to work the spit. After some time, however, she left to attend to other chores. When she returned, she found to her great shock that Catherine, still in ecstasy, had fallen over into some live coals. Terrified, Lisa pulled Catherine from the fire, but to her great surprise found that neither Catherine's body nor her clothes had been the least bit affected, even though she had been lying on the fire for several minutes. (CS, ?)

God the Father told Catherine: "Hereafter they [converted souls] know that all labor in this life is small, on account of the shortness of time. Time is as the point of a needle and no more, and when time has passed, labor is ended. Therefore you see that the labor is small." (CS, 128)

God the Father said to Catherine: "This love [of the world] so dazzles the eye of the intellect that it can discern and see nothing but such glittering objects. It is the very brightness of the things that causes the intellect to perceive them and the affection to love them. For had worldly things no such brightness, there would be no sin, for man, by his nature, cannot desire anything but good, and vice, appearing to him thus, under color of the soul's good, causes him to sin." (CS, 131–132)

God the Father said to Catherine: "Most of those who enter [religious life—i.e., a convent or monastery] are imperfect. There are some who enter already in perfection. Others [are] in the childhood of virtue, others through fear, others through penance, others through allurements. Everything [regarding their progress] depends on whether, after they have entered, they exercise themselves in virtue and persevere until death. For no true judgment can be made on a person's entrance into religion except by their perseverance. Many have appeared to be perfect who have either afterwards turned back or remained in the order with much imperfection." (CS, 295)

Many saints have written about how holy it is to be in prayer, but holier still is to leave prayer in order to perform an act of charity. God the Father spoke regarding those who find themselves in prayer but another matter calls for attention. "You should never leave prayer, except for necessity, charity, or obedience." (CS, 323)

Jesus said to Saint Bridget of Sweden: "It was from My Spirit, through infusion, that all My evangelists had the words that they spoke and wrote." (BS, 66)

Jesus said to Bridget, "Some [evangelists] wrote things that they had heard but had not seen. Others wrote earlier things later. Some wrote more about My divinity. And each one wrote just as the Holy Spirit enabled him to speak. However, I want you to know that acceptance is to be given only to those evangelists whom My Church accepts. Many who had zeal tried to write, but not in accordance with My own knowledge." (BS, 150)

Jesus told Bridget to relay the following message to the queen of Cyprus, "She is to put down the shameful custom of women involving tight clothing, display of the breasts, unguents and many other vanities, for these are things entirely hateful to

God. She should have a confessor who, having left the world, loves souls more than gifts and who neither glosses over sins nor fears to reprove them. And, in those things that pertain to the salvation of the soul, she is to obey him just as she obeys God." (BS, 193)

Brother Gerekin heard in spirit the following words concerning Bridget: "This is the woman who, coming from the ends of the earth, shall give countless nations wisdom to drink." (BS, 80)

Saint John the Baptist said to Bridget, "Because you wept over the fact that your son offended me by not fasting on my vigil, and because you would prefer him to serve me rather than be a king, I shall therefore help him and shall arm him with my arms." (BS, 76)

Margaret's abstinence and austerities weakened her body so much that her confessor urged her to relax their severity. She told him there could be no truce in the conflict between body and soul. She cried out to God, telling Him she would "die to this mortal life a thousand times a day." *He replied,* "My child, you shall tell all this to your confessor: that in this life no Christian can be perfect who does not restrain his bodily appetite, for without abstinence from food and drink the war of the flesh will never end and those who refuse this saving remedy suffer most from the rebellion of the flesh." (MC, 131–132)

Jesus said to Bridget, "Friend, the ugliness and the beauty of this world are like bitterness and sweetness. The ugliness of the world—its contempt and its adversity—is a profitable sort of bitterness that heals the just. The world's beauty [i.e.

what people are attracted to] is its prosperity, and this is a flattering sort of sweetness, but false and seductive. Therefore, he who flees the beauty of the world and spits out its sweetness will not come to the ugliness of Hell or taste its bitterness, but will ascend to My joy. . . . In order to escape the ugliness of Hell and to acquire the sweetness of Heaven, it is necessary to go after the world's ugliness rather than its beauty. For even though all things were well created by Me and are all very good, nevertheless, one must beware especially of those things which can furnish an occasion for the loss of souls . . ." (BS, 110)

Jesus, speaking to all of us, said: "Death will be hard for you, judgment unendurable and flight impossible, unless you amend yourself." (BS, 133)

The Virgin Mary said to Bridget, "In that place [the nearby Franciscan monastery] there are two kinds of human beings. Some love God with all their hearts; others want to have God, but the world is sweeter to them than God is." (BS, 194)

Jesus said to Bridget, "O My Rome! O My Rome! The Pope scorns you and does not attend to My words, but accepts the doubtful in place of the certain. Therefore he shall hear My pipe [the words of Bridget] no more, for he makes the time of My mercy dependent on his own choice." (BS, 218)

Jesus said to Bridget: "There are very few who reflect upon the charity of My Passion and of My patience." (BS, 93)

Saint Margaret of Cortona prayed one day to Jesus, asking that she might be granted permission to speak about the special graces he was giving her: "I beg of You, my Lord God, that as

You have healed my soul by the sweetness of Your presence, so now You will bury Your handmaid from the world and never permit me to speak of the secret things which You reveal to me in ecstasy." *The Lord replied:* "Margaret, it belongs to Me to say whether you shall keep silence or speak. Behold, I have given you My apostles, the Friars Minor, who shall preach abroad what things I have done in you, even as the apostles preached My Gospel to all nations." (MC, 146–148)

On a feast day of the Purification of the Mother of God, Margaret hungered to receive Holy Communion. But she was afraid to receive Jesus in the sacred Host because she felt she must be displeasing to Him since He no longer consoled her with feelings of His presence upon receiving the great Sacrament. Her spiritual director then commanded her to receive Holy Communion, so she received Our Lord, but still found no consolation. She became deeply afraid and began crying. Jesus then spoke to her, "My child, don't be astonished that you did not feel more quickly the joy of My presence. When you came to receive Me, your soul was not fully prepared. I [wish to] give Myself to you in such a way that you are prepared to receive Me."

Margaret answered Him, "Lord, I was afraid to receive You because it seemed to me that my soul was not prepared for so high a guest."

Jesus said to her, "My child, it pleased Me that you should receive Me, and in giving Myself to you and drawing you to Me, I give Myself to the mother of sinners. For I have made you to be as a mother to those who have sinned. And in keeping you away from Me it is as though the evil one had kept Me from My own mother."

Margaret could hardly contain herself upon hearing these words. Jesus continued: "As the most Blessed Virgin was chosen to be My mother according to the flesh for the sake of all mankind, so you are chosen to be in your own fashion a mirror for sinners, and their mother. For by My grace you have become most beautiful before Me in Heaven, and I will make you holy upon the earth."

Margaret continued to wonder why at times she would experience the strength and consolation of Christ's presence, then at other times she would feel nothing. Jesus addressed this as well: "You find Me just as I find you. In these days your mind is distracted, weary with many labors. Look at Mary Magdalene. I showed Myself to her in the garden after my Resurrection in such a way that I was already in her soul. But now I have put you in the world to be a ladder by which sinners shall mount to Me."

Margaret replied "Lord, what can sinners see in me for their example?"

Jesus answered her, "They will imitate your abstinences and fasts, your humility and patience in suffering, your gentleness of speech, and your meekness. They will imitate, too, your sincerity and the solicitude with which you shun the world." (MC, 241–244)

Suffering

One day Jesus said to Saint Margaret of Cortona, "You are My child because you are obedient to Me; you are My spouse because you love Me alone; you are My mother when according to your strength you do My Father's will. . . . Yet presume not on these words, for you still have to pay a price for these consolations greater than you have hitherto paid. The time is coming when in your own sufferings you will learn how great a price I, your Redeemer, paid for you." (MC, 145)

In anguish, Margaret asked Jesus when she would finally be able to be separated from this world and return to Him. He answered her, "As long as it pleases Me you shall remain upon the earth, and in so far as it is possible to a human body, you must buy your crown before you can obtain it. Therefore you [should] still be prepared to suffer." *Margaret asked:* "You have promised me so many inestimable gifts, Lord, and yet you will not give me entire confidence." *Jesus responded,* "I tell you, this entire confidence which you seek, you cannot have while you are in this life."

"I ask for it," *Margaret said,* "so that I may not doubt and be deceived."

To this, Jesus said, "You shall not be deceived in regard to My promises. This I tell you."

"Lord," *Margaret said,* "it is not for myself that I seek this, but rather because of the faith of those who, on account of me, will praise and serve and desire You. For, my Lord, whatever I love or desire, I love and desire for You and not for myself, unworthy and vile creature that I am." *Jesus said:* "Yes, you love, and you shall be loved; you serve and you shall be served; and as you desire to glorify and obey Me, so too you shall be desired, glorified, and obeyed." (MC, 214–215)

God the Father told Saint Catherine of Siena, "Consider that the love of divine charity is so closely joined in the soul with perfect patience [that] neither can leave the soul without the other. For this reason, if the soul chooses to love Me, she should also choose to endure pains for Me in whatever mode or circumstance I may send them to her. Patience cannot be proved in any other way than by suffering. Patience is united with love as has been said. Therefore, bear yourselves with manly courage. Unless you do so, you will not prove yourselves to be spouses of My Truth, My faithful children." (CS, 39)

God the Father told Catherine "Very pleasing to Me, dearest daughter, is the willing desire to bear every pain and fatigue, even to death, for the salvation of souls. The more the soul endures, the more she shows that she loves Me. In loving Me she comes to know more of My truth, [and] the more she knows, the more pain and intolerable grief she feels at the offenses committed against Me." (CS, 38)

Referring to the fact that every person must carry a cross in life, God the Father told Catherine: "No one can pass through this life without a cross, far less those who travel by the lower way [i.e. souls who reject conversion]. Not that My servants pass without pain, but their pain is alleviated." (CS, 124)

God the Father said to Catherine: "I wish you to know that all the sufferings that creatures endure depend on their will, because if their will were in accordance with Mine, they would endure no suffering. . . . [The torments that a converted soul endures] cause no suffering to a will that gladly endures them, seeing that they are ordained by My will." (CS, 258)

Sister Katherine of Mount St. Mary said to Saint Bridget of Sweden, "O you happy lady! For I am not speaking so that either you or I would be boasting, because I have heard for very certain a voice that said this: 'Know that Bridget shall yet be called happy, because, if she is scorned on earth, she will be honored in Heaven and those to be born will proclaim her name.' Therefore, stand firm, because without doubt it will thus be accomplished, even as I have heard." (BS, 80)

Fridays were very emotional and sad days for Margaret, and especially on Good Fridays she was like a mother who had lost her son. One Good Friday, languishing in the depths of depression, she was weeping over Jesus' Passion when He spoke to her: "Margaret, if you were in a deep, woody solitude on a dark night, surrounded by all manner of dangers, would you hesitate to come to Me?"

Margaret quickly responded that she would be like a little child running to its mother. Jesus answered her, "My child, why do you seek to find a paradise here on earth when I denied it to My own body, united though it was to my Divinity? You must not hope for this, because on no account can it be granted to you. You are like Peter, who having beheld My glory on Tabor, wished in the intoxication of his soul to build three tabernacles there, and to dwell in that place because of the sweetness which filled his being. His desire was not granted to him. Neither can you possess here on earth the paradise I have promised you hereafter." (MC, 192–193)

Margaret had been in another deep desolation when she called out to Jesus, saying that her soul could find no peace. Jesus at once responded: "My child, I am your Savior who called you back from the way of death, first when I hung upon the Cross and again when I called you to do penance, even as I once called Matthew and Magdalene. As these [two] followed Me faithfully after their conversion, so shall you follow after Me and be vilified and spoken against by many. Nevertheless, it is not by a martyr's blood that you shall go forth from this world as did My apostle.

"And just as they murmured against Magdalene because she cast aside her ornaments and followed Me, so shall men deride you for following Me. For though your sufferings may increase, so too shall My grace increase in you, and I will that you shall tell your confessor to signify to Fra Giovanni [*Fra*

Giovanni da Castiglione, Margaret's chief spiritual director] that he earnestly pray for you, inasmuch as your sufferings will be great and suspicion will surround you. Even they themselves will sometimes doubt you, and many will doubt you until your death. But in the end I will make all things clear and you shall leave behind you comfort and blessings for many." (MC, 194–196)

One Saturday Margaret received the Body of Our Lord in the Most Holy Eucharist and was filled with a great joy. Because of her many penances she was very weak and was not able to stand up. She then heard Jesus ask her to lay her head upon a pillow and talk with Him. He said to her: "Do you believe that I, the eternal and one God, am Father, Son, and Holy Spirit?

Margaret agreed with Him, whereupon Jesus continued "My child, even so did I question My apostle Peter, because I delight in the loving converse of My friends."

Margaret then inquired of Jesus, "How can you find delight in creatures, since Your delight is already such that it can be neither diminished nor increased?" Jesus responded to her: "Does Scripture not say that My delight is to be with the children of men? But in you I act as I do [so that I can] afflict in you the enemy who, being himself shut out from the joys of paradise, seeks incessantly to afflict Me by taking from souls their joy."

Margaret responded that her sufferings were insignificant because of her love for Him. To this, Jesus answered, "Much do I delight in pure love."

When she heard this, Margaret made a request, "Lord, teach me to love You with a pure love, for no one can have this except from You, the source of all good things."

Jesus replied, "Do you want Me to make known to you the marks of pure love which are in you?"

Margaret replied yes, and Jesus answered, "Are you willing to die for My sake? Is it not sweet to you to fast continually and to shed tears of sorrow for the honor of My name? Have you not chosen most strict poverty for love of Me who was poor and needy? Do you not shun all worldly conversation that you may more readily commune with Me alone? Is there any pain you would refuse in your love of Me?" (MC, 198–200)

Margaret was meditating one day on Jesus' Passion when she heard Him say, "Prepare yourself for struggle and suffering, for you will have hardships and troubles as long as you live. For as gold is cleansed in the furnace, so will I cleanse you by tribulation and temptation and sickness, by sorrow and fear, by watching and tears, by hunger and thirst, cold and nakedness. But when you are cleansed, you shall pass into eternal joy. But let no fear of these things terrify you; act bravely and gladly bear all things, because I am with you in all your tribulations. And that you may not faint in your difficult way, I will often refresh you by the joy of My presence." (MC, 172–175)

As Margaret was pondering the insults Christ was subjected to, she heard His voice, saying, "My child, grievous indeed to you is the bodily weakness which by My will is little by little consuming you. Grievous too is the persistence of temptation; yet grievous above all and most painful is it when I take from you My consolations or delay to comfort you. But do not be troubled or astonished because temptations come to you, for the more I fill you with delights, so much more does the enemy of souls endeavor out of envy to wound you with the darts of his temptations." (MC, 172–175)

The Lord said to Margaret, "Remember that as My favors increase in you, so shall your sufferings increase." (MC, 154)

Jesus said to Bridget, "My Passion was to Me more bitter than a puncture in the eye, yet I suffered it out of charity. My mother's sorrow moved My heart more than My own, yet I bore it. For a long time, all My inner and outer parts trembled out of pressing pain and suffering, and yet I did not dismiss it or draw back." (BS, 132–133)

Jesus appeared to Bridget and spoke to her regarding a boy named Benedict and the cause of his illness, "This boy's infirmity has not been caused by constellations of stars—as the foolish say—nor by his sins. He has become infirm because of his physical condition and so that his crown will be greater." (BS, 89)

The Holy Spirit said to Bridget, "The Devil hates the tears of good people, which proceed from divine charity." (BS, 89)

Jesus said to Bridget, "As to why all things are born with suffering, I answer: 'When man [Adam] scorned the most beautiful delight, he immediately incurred a toilsome life. . . . Therefore, man is born with pain and makes progress with labor so that he may be eager to hasten to his true rest." (BS, 140)

The Virgin Mary appeared to Bridget and said, "I am the Queen of those in misery." (BS, 79)

One Saturday, after receiving the Body and Blood of Christ, Margaret had a discussion with Jesus, who said to her, "My child, separate yourself as far as you can from all interactions with people except the Friars Minor [the Franciscans]. To others, your many afflictions may seem light and of no consequence. But to you suffering them, they are indeed heavy and full of pain. And even if you do not suffer all you wish to, still bear sweetly and with a calm mind for love of Me such sufferings as come to you. But your interior struggles, wherein your soul is being made beautiful—those struggles, which are more bitter to you than death, shall be accounted to you for the martyr's palm."

Margaret answered that she felt that her soul could not be cleansed or made beautiful by such sufferings. Jesus answered, "What you say is true, of themselves these sufferings could not cleanse or beautify your soul. But your love, your faithfulness in trials, and My mercy—these are what cleanse and beautify. And be aware that though you suffer much because of your temptations and your infirmities and your good works, yet even so I protect you. Never again will you offend Me by grievous sin."

Later, on the night following the Feast of Saint Benedict, Margaret was weeping bitterly because of her compassion for one of the friars who was having great difficulties. Jesus informed her, "Tell him to prepare his soul, for this is not his last trouble. He shall be tried by troubles within and without, and he shall so taste My Passion that he'll fear he must surely fall. Nevertheless, let him find comfort in Me, for I will strengthen his patience that he may not fall, and in the end he will stand in good stead."

On another day, which was the Feast of the Finding of the Head of Saint John the Baptist, upon receiving the Body of the Lord, Margaret heard Christ say to her: "You have petitioned that I bless My friars and I, the Redeemer of all, bless them all together by the love of the elect in whose company they are. But tell the superiors, My vicars, that they must prepare themselves for troubles, since the Friars Minor, closer than all others upon the earth, imitate Me.

"Yet, let them be comforted, for I will be with them. And although I bless others too, yet to them I give a special blessing because for My sake they did not turn away from faithfully caring for you, My poor sheep whom I brought back to the sheepfold. You tell Me, poor sheep, that you were long in coming. But I tell you that one day of reconciliation and grace is [worth] more than a year, or a hundred years, without grace." (MC, 210–212; 213–214)

Trials and Temptations

God the Father said to Saint Catherine of Siena, "My love permits temptations, for the Devil is weak and by himself can do nothing unless I allow him. And I let him tempt through love and not through hatred, that you may conquer [your passions] and not that you may be conquered. . . . Not that it is the intention of the Devil to prove virtue in you, for he has no love, but rather to deprive you of it, and this he cannot do if you do not wish it." (CS, 119, 120)

God the Father said to Catherine, "Only those who feel themselves to be alone, who hope only in themselves, deprived of the affection of love, fear and are afraid of every little thing." (CS, 252)

Jesus said to Saint Bridget of Sweden, "Many [people] work in manly ways with prayers and good deeds in order to reach Heaven, but when they think they have attained the peace of being with God, they get involved in temptations, their troubles increase, and just as they envisage themselves perfect, they discover that they are totally imperfect." (BS, 44)

During her prayers, Bridget was sometimes tempted with unclean thoughts. The Blessed Virgin Mary appeared to her and said, "The Devil is like an envious spy, seeking to accuse and impede the good. Therefore try and pray as long as you are being tempted because your desire and good effort will count for you as prayer; and if you cannot cast out of your mind the sordid matters that come to it, those efforts will count for you as merit provided that you not consent and as these things are against your will." (BS, 62)

Jesus said to Bridget, "For some, temptations increase in the beginning of their conversion to the spiritual life; and such persons are more perfectly strengthened in the end. Others are more gravely tempted in the middle of their lives and at the end. These must look to themselves carefully, never having any presumption about themselves, but laboring all the more bravely. . . . Therefore, daughter, you are not to marvel if even [in] old age, temptations increase. For as long as life is permitted, temptation too is possible." (BS, 127)

Jesus said to Bridget, "Behold, daughter, how greatly there prevails in man not only the Devil's malice but also a depraved conscience! This comes about from the fact that man does not wrestle against his temptations as he ought." (BS, 151)

Jesus said to Saint Bridget, "For three reasons tribulation comes to human beings: either for greater humility—as when King David was troubled; or for greater fear and caution—as when Sarah, Abraham's wife, was taken away by the king; or for a human being's greater consolation and honor." (BS, 163)

Jesus said to Bridget, "Be diligently attentive to yourself!" *Bridget answered,* "Why?" *Jesus said,* "Because the world is sending to you four servants who wish to deceive you.

The first is the worry of riches. When he comes, answer him: 'Riches are transitory, and the greater their abundance, the greater the accounting of them that one must give. Therefore, I do not care about them because they do not follow their owner, but leave him.'

The second servant is the loss of riches and the deprivation of things that had been bestowed. Answer him thus: 'He who gave the riches has Himself taken them away. He knows what is expedient for me. May His will be done!'

The third servant is the tribulation of this world. Speak to him thus: 'Blessed be You, my God, who permits me to be troubled. For through tribulations I know that I belong to You because You permit tribulation in the present that You may spare in the future. Therefore, distribute to me patience and strength to endure.'

The fourth servant is scorn and insults. Answer them thus: 'God alone is good, and to Him all honor is due. But I, who have done all wicked and worthless deeds, whence or why should I have honor? I am worthy, rather, of every insult because the whole of my life has blasphemed God. Why does honor mean more to me than insult? For it only excites pride and diminishes humility, and God is forgotten. Therefore, to God be all honor and praise.' For the sake of these reasons, stand fast against the servants of the world, and love Me, your God, with all your heart." (BS, 123–124)

Regarding the crowning of a new king, Jesus said to Bridget, "In ancient times, kingdoms were well ruled when such a man was elected as king—one who had the will and the knowledge and the ability to rule with justice. Now kingdoms are not kingdoms but the scenes of childishness, folly, and brigandage. . . . Woe to that kingdom whose king is a child, who lives daintily and has dainty flatterers but feels no anguish at all about the advancement of the community." (BS, ?)

Because of thoughts of her own unworthiness, Saint Margaret of Cortona would often refrain from receiving Holy Communion. One day, taking pity on her, Jesus said to her, "My child, do not abstain from receiving the Sacrament of My Body as you have been doing. You are already so far cleansed from vice that I command you to receive Me often.

"[At those times] due to sickness when you are unable to bear the burden of prayer as you were accustomed to in the first days of your conversion, [it is enough to confess] your sins and avoid worldly conversation.

"Love silence. If you can confess your sins before breaking your fast, do so. Don't hide your life from the friars, your confessors, so you won't be deceived by any temptation."

After receiving Holy Communion on another day, Margaret was thinking about why Jesus would lower Himself to come down to our level. She asked Him, "Why, O Lord, did You humble Yourself so greatly at Your Last Supper to Judas and the others. Why do You continue even now to give Yourself to us?"

The Lord answered Margaret, "My child, truly today there are many Judases to whom it is permitted to receive Me and to touch Me. But you, out of your love for Me, have stripped yourself often and made yourself a beggar. So I will clothe you with grace and enrich your soul. And now do not fear whatever tribulation may come upon you, because in your tribulations you are made acceptable to Me and united to Me in love." (MC, ?)

Seeing that Margaret was filled with great peace, the Devil began to fill her with doubts, putting it into her mind that her whole life was a deception. Margaret begged the Lord to guard her against the enemy. Christ comforted her, saying, "Does My child think the deceiver could give you the good things I give you, or that anyone can enter into your soul as I, the Creator, have? How could he who is without joy give you joy? But if he could, he would take away your joy because he himself has none. I, your salvation, will not permit you to be deceived." (MC, 119–120)

Virtue

God the Father said to Saint Catherine of Siena, "Justice is not diminished by the wicked man's injustice, but is rather proved . . . I say also to you that, not only is virtue proved in those who render good for evil, but that many times a good man gives back fiery coals of love, which dispel the hatred and rancor of the heart of the angry. From hatred often comes benevolence by virtue of the love and perfect patience which is in him who sustains the anger of the wicked, bearing and supporting his defects. If you will observe the virtues of fortitude and perseverance, these virtues are proved by the long endurance of the injuries and detractions of wicked men. Whether by injuries or by flattery, [these evil types] constantly endeavor to turn a man aside from following the road and the doctrine of Truth." (CS, 49)

God the Father said to Catherine, "Labor to increase the fire of your desire, and do not let a moment pass without crying to Me with humble voice, or without continual prayers before Me for your neighbors. I say this to you and to the father of your soul [her confessor] whom I have given you on earth. Bear yourselves with manful courage and make yourselves dead to all your own sensuality." (CS, 38)

God the Father said to Catherine, "If virtue were not visible and did not shine in the time of trial, it would not have been truly conceived." (CS, 60)

Miscellaneous

God the Father said to Saint Catherine of Siena: "By His death [Jesus] destroyed every vice, so that no one could say that any vice remained that was not punished and beaten out with pains. . . ." (CS, 99–100)

God the Father said to Catherine: "My creatures should see and know that I wish nothing but their good through the Blood of My only-begotten Son, in which they are washed from their iniquities. By this Blood they are enabled to know My Truth. In order to give them eternal life, I created them in My image and likeness, and recreated them to grace with the Blood of My Son, making them sons of adoption." (CS, 143–144)

Catherine was illiterate during the early years of her religious life. Alessia Saracini gave her lessons in order to be able to read her breviary, which was her great desire, but despite the lessons Catherine was still unable to read. In her exasperation she resigned herself to simply saying the Our Father and Hail Mary like other illiterate women of her age. Her desire to read and write, though, was suddenly given to her one day miraculously, as was testified by her contemporaries as well as Catherine herself. Friar Thomas of Siena related:

"Catherine learned to write miraculously: one day, on coming from mental prayer, she wrote to Etienne Maconi a letter which concluded thus: 'You must know, my beloved son, that this is the first letter I ever wrote myself.' Etienne

Maconi certifies that she wrote many after, and that several pages of the book that she composed are written with her own hand."

In another letter, Catherine wrote: "I wrote this letter myself, and the one that I already sent you. For God gave me the facility to write, so that when coming forth from ecstasy I might discharge my heart . . ." *God grants to souls wisdom in order to enlighten the mind. God the Father told Saint Catherine that love follows the intellect, and that with this light of God, souls can then love God:* "The more [the intellect] knows, the more it can love." (CS, 185)

God the Father said to Catherine: "The soul who lives virtuously places the root of her tree in the valley of true humility. But those who live miserably are planted on the mountain of pride. . . . No good actions done by a soul in mortal sin are of value for eternal life since they are not done in grace. Yet, a soul should not abandon its good works on this account, because every good deed is rewarded, and every evil deed [is] punished." (CS, 200)

Jesus said to Saint Bridget of Sweden: "One who possesses a meadow does not spare the meadow in preference to his laboring horse. So I, the Lord, provide for My friends when their own providence fails, and I stir up the souls of others to do good to them." (BS, 92)

God the Father said to Bridget: "Although man's intellect is darkened, nevertheless there is no shadow or change in Me. I do arrange, and have arranged, all things so temperately and honestly and wisely that nothing has been made without a cause or use, not the highest mountain, nor the desert, nor the lakes; not the beasts, nor even the venomous reptiles. I provide for the usefulness of all creatures as well as of mankind." (BS, 144)

ABOUT THE AUTHOR

Craig Turner is a journalist who covered Capitol Hill for a Washington, D.C. news organization during the 1980s. Since then he has also been a writer of magazine and newspaper articles on a variety of issues, including financial matters, cultural issues and religion. He lives in Burke, Virginia, with his wife and three rowdy boys.

TAN · BOOKS

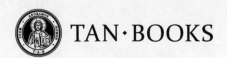

TAN Books was founded in 1967 to preserve the spiritual, intellectual and liturgical traditions of the Catholic Church. At a critical moment in history TAN kept alive the great classics of the Faith and drew many to the Church. In 2008 TAN was acquired by Saint Benedict Press. Today TAN continues its mission to a new generation of readers.

From its earliest days TAN has published a range of booklets that teach and defend the Faith. Through partnerships with organizations, apostolates, and mission-minded individuals, well over 10 million TAN booklets have been distributed.

More recently, TAN has expanded its publishing with the launch of Catholic calendars and daily planners—as well as Bibles, fiction, and multimedia products through its sister imprints Catholic Courses (CatholicCourses.com) and Saint Benedict Press (SaintBenedictPress.com).

Today TAN publishes over 500 titles in the areas of theology, prayer, devotions, doctrine, Church history, and the lives of the saints. TAN books are published in multiple languages and found throughout the world in schools, parishes, bookstores and homes.

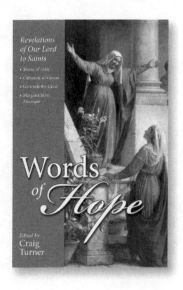

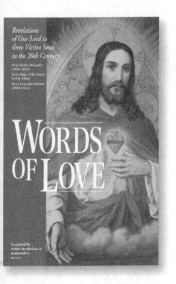

TAN·CLASSICS

A collection of the finest literature in the Catholic tradition.

978-0-89555-227-3

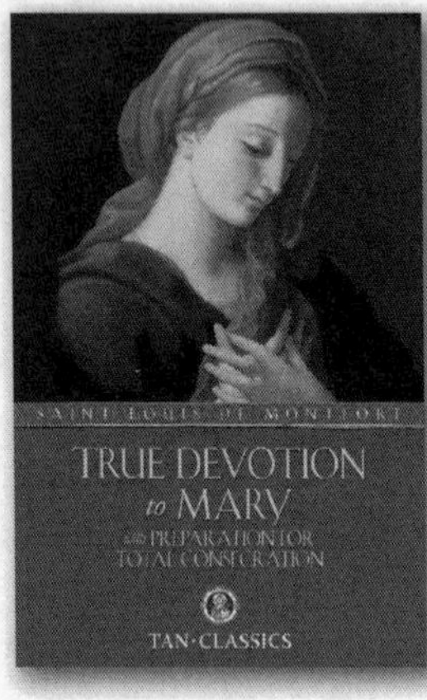

978-0-89555-154-2

978-0-89555-155-9

Our TAN Classics collection is a well-balanced sampling of the finest literature in the Catholic tradition.

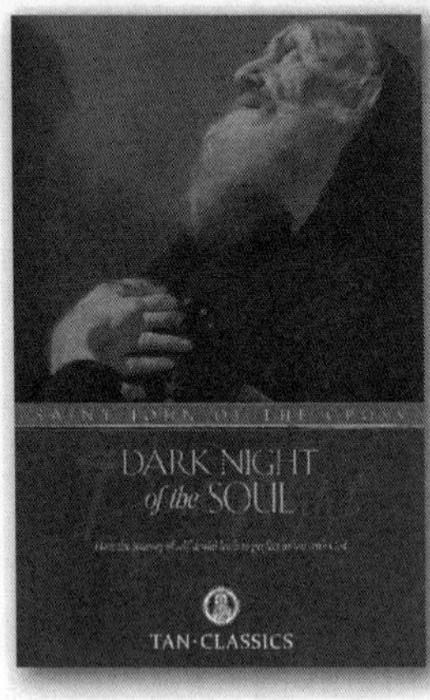

978-0-89555-230-3

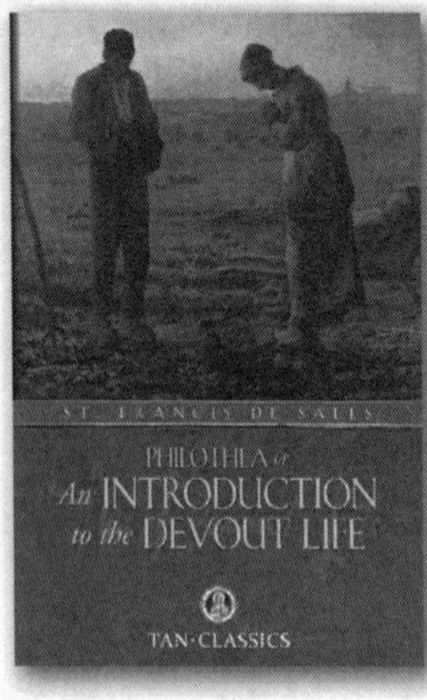

978-0-89555-228-0

978-0-89555-151-1

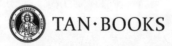

TAN·BOOKS

78-0-89555-153-5

978-0-89555-149-8

978-0-89555-199-3

The collection includes distinguished spiritual works of the saints, philosophical treatises and famous biographies.

78-0-89555-226-6

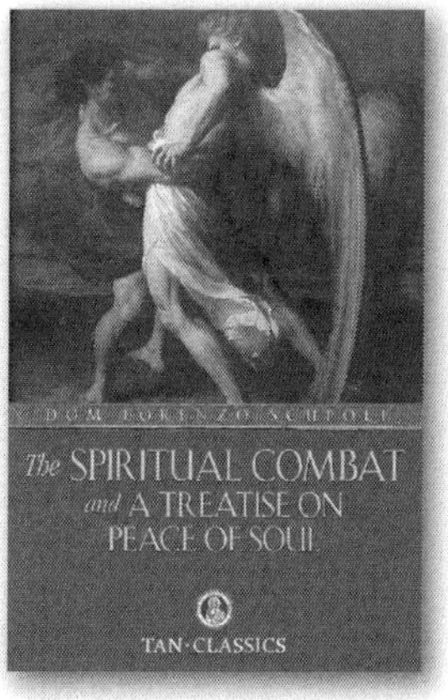

978-0-89555-152-8

978-0-89555-225-9

Visit us at TANBooks.com